The

Book

of

Awesome

The

Book

of

Awesome

Neil Pasricha

hardie grant books
MELBOURNE · LONDON

Published in Australia in 2010 by
Hardie Grant Books
85 High Street
Prahran, Victoria 3181, Australia
www.hardiegrant.com.au

First published in the USA in 2010 by
Amy Einhorn Books/Putnam
An imprint of Penguin Books
375 Hudson Street
New York, New York 10014, USA
www.penguin.com

Cataloguing-in-Publication data is available from the National Library of Australia.
The Book of Awesome
ISBN 978 1 74066 879 8

Cover design by Design by Committee
Text design by Amanda Dewey
Printed and bound in China by C & C Offset Printing

All photographs by Sam Javanrouh (dailydoseofimagery.com) with exception of "Wordless Apologies" by Evan Long, "Smiling and Thinking of Good Friends Who Are Gone" by Dina Kim, and "When the Vending Machine Gives You Two Things Instead of One" and "The Perfect Chicken Wing Partner" by iStockphoto.

Completely swallowing and devouring up every tiny last word of the entire book, including all the copyright, printing and library cataloguing data that nobody usually reads. AWESOME!

The

Book

of

Awesome

So what's this all about?

....

Polar ice caps are melting, **hurricanes swirl in the seas**, wars are heating up around the world, and the job market is in a deep freeze.

Whoa.

It's getting pretty ugly out there.

That's why one chilly spring night I started a tiny website called **1000 Awesome Things**. For a boring guy with a nine-to-five job, it became a getaway from my everyday.

I never imagined that writing about **finding money in your old coat pocket**, the smell of gasoline, or watching *The Price Is Right* when you're at home sick would amount to anything.

Honestly, when I started the site I got excited when my mom forwarded it to my dad and the traffic doubled. Then I got excited when friends sent it to friends and strangers started sending me suggestions: **"When cashiers open up new checkout lanes at the grocery store,"** "The smell of rain on a hot sidewalk," "Waking up and realizing it's Saturday."

It seems like maybe these tiny little moments make an awesome difference in many of our rushed, jam-packed lives. Maybe we all love snow days, peeling an orange in one shot, and **Popping Bubble Wrap.**

Maybe we're basically all the same.

Over the past year the website grew into a warm place where people around the world came to **curl up under a blanket** and think about the small joys we often overlook. With so much sad news and bad news pouring down upon us, it's fun to stop for a minute and share a universal high five with the rest of humanity.

What started on a whim has changed me for the better too. Now when I get the thank-you wave while merging, **hear the crack of ice cubes in my drink**, or move clothes from the washer to the dryer without dropping anything, I just smile and enjoy the moment.

So . . . that's the story so far. That's how we got from there to here. And now it's time to come on in. The fire's crackling and there's a seat on the couch here. Cuddle up and let's all get into it.

Let's all get onto it.

And let's all get a little bit

AWESOME!

The other side of the pillow

....

Have you ever found yourself lying in bed **wide awake** in the middle of the night?

You know how it is: **Clock's clicking** past 1:30 a.m. and you lie there with your eyes bugged open, chewing your upper lip, tapping the sheets with your fingers, completely frustrated. Your pupils have long adjusted to the dark, so your eyes are darting around the room over and over, trying to identify dark shapes or watching the moonlight shadow-dance around the walls. Maybe your thoughts won't settle down, you just can't get comfortable, **you ate spicy food** before bed, you have a presentation the next morning, or maybe it's just the frustration itself keeping you in a terrible, never-ending cycle of sleeplessness.

So you **play dead** and try to remain motionless as long as possible. You change positions back and forth, side to side, left to right. You get up and go to the bathroom or start reading a book. Maybe you try to remake the bed, since by now you've probably managed to twist your sheets and blankets into a completely unusable, tightly wound knotpile barely covering your legs.

On nights like this, when you just can't sleep, one of the greatest things invented is simply **Turning Over the Pillow**.

Yes, flipping over your pillow and checking out the other side cranks **Bed Comfort** up a few notches and is a simple and easy way to help you relax and get comfy.

The other side of the pillow, folks. Because it's flat when you're sagging, **fresh when you're stale**, and cold when you're hot, baby.

AWESOME!

When cashiers open up new checkout lanes at the grocery store

Though I hate to admit it, I am a slow, indecisive mess in the grocery store checkout lane.

Since I am an **extremely cheap person**, I watch the prices scroll up on screen like a hawk, often saying things like "Oh, I thought that was on sale," or "Actually, I don't really want that anymore," forcing the cashier to call in price checks to the unresponsive produce department or find a temporary home for the pack of **melting Fudgsicles** I've decided to leave off my list last minute.

And because I'm watching the screen so closely, I start bagging my groceries late, fumble with my wallet, and awkwardly leave my shopping cart blocking the lane like a metal **crisscrossed castle knight** enforcing a firm "Thou shall not pass" law in its trademark silence.

Yes, I clog up the line and annoy everybody behind me. I'm one of **Four People You Don't Want to Stand Behind** in the grocery line, together with:

- **Fidgety Grandma**, who on cue dumps a pile of warm nickels on the counter to pay and then slowly

counts them out by sliding them across the counter
with her index finger

- **Flyer Guy**, who hands the cashier a dog-eared flyer
  from home, forcing her to manually tear out all
  the coupons while everybody waits
- **No-Math Jack**, who sneaks in piles of extra items into
  the Express Lane and acts like it's no big deal

Those tense, winding checkout lanes can be a pretty
rough go sometimes. It's not easy out there. You have to
watch the anxiety levels, take deep breaths, keep that blood
pressure in check.

That's why there are few things better than a **sprightly
new cashier** hopping onto the scene, grabbing the "Next lane
please" sign from the end of the belt, flicking on the lightbulb above her station, and offering a loud, beaming "Next
customer, please!" to the scowling, stressed-out masses.

When that cashier bulb goes on, a **bright warm glow** showers down on everybody waiting. People like me feel less
guilty about holding up the line and folks at the end win the
big front-of-the-line jackpot. Yes, it's **one giant mood swing**,
one massive swelling of goodwill, complete with buzzing
chatter, a few laughs, and even the occasional crinkly plastic
sound of a tightly wound frown turning upside down.

AWESOME!

Wearing underwear just out of the dryer

....

Now tell me: Is there anything quite so nice as wrapping yourself up in a pair of steaming skivvies just out of the dryer? It's like skinny-dipping in a hot tub, jumping on a horse that's been in the sun all day, and lying on a warm, sandy beach . . . combined! Sure, the moment doesn't last long, yes, there may be some static cling, and it's true, you'll have to get changed really quickly in the laundry room to pull it off.

But dang, girl.

Hot undies, they is fine.

AWESOME!

Old, dangerous playground equipment

....

Slides used to be dangerous.

After climbing up those **sandy, metal crosstrax steps**, you got to the top and stared down at that steep ride below. The slide was burning hot to the touch, a stovetop set too high all day under the summer sun, just waiting to greet the underside of your legs with first-degree burns as you enjoyed the ride. It also smelled like hot pee, years of nervous children with leaky nappies permanently marking it as their territory. Lastly, to top it all off, there were no cute plastic side rails or encapsulated tube slides, which meant that if you went too fast or aimed your legs poorly, your shoes would **grip-skid on the metal**, and you'd spill over the side, landing face down with a sickening thud in a bed of pebbles, cigarette butts, and milk thistles.

It wasn't just slides either. Everything in the playground was more dangerous. And it was different and unique, seemingly put together by the **neighborhood handymen** who in a burst of creative energy one Saturday morning emptied their garages of old tires, two-by-fours, and chains and just nailed them all together.

There were wooden tightrope beams suspended high in

the air, daring the confident, athletic kids to attempt a slow, heart-pounding high-wire walk while other kids encouragingly showered them with handfuls of sand and **pinecones**.

There were fire poles two stories high—just cheap, simple poles planted deep in the ground that were popular **and educational**, quietly introducing children to concepts like gravity, friction, and badly sprained ankles. There was a certain Fire Pole Form too, a kind of arms-on, cross-legged, spider-wrap maneuver that was both awkward and majestic at the same time.

And of course, there was my favorite: the **Big Spinner**, also known as a **Merry-Go-Round**. This was just a giant metal circle that lay a foot off the ground and could be spun, usually by someone standing beside it. If you were lucky, you'd get a pile of kids on there and somebody's mom or dad would kindly whip you into a **World of Unimaginable Dizziness**. A couple kids would fly off from the g-forces, but most would hang on, teeth gritted, eyes squinted, cheeks flapping wildly against the wind, until the Big Spinner reluctantly came to a slow stop and finally let everyone off. Kids would walk away in different directions, some hitting tree trunks head-on, others falling down nearby hills.

These days those classic playgrounds sure are hard to come by.

Everything is plastic now, unaffected by temperature, easy to disinfect, and bendable into all kinds of **Safe-T-Shapes**—the sharp, rusty nail heads of yesterday replaced with nontoxic washable adhesives poured from a cauldron of polymers and Purell. Now not only are our kids getting lame **baby-approved fun**, but just think what we're doing to the tetanus shot industry.

Seriously though, new playgrounds sure are terrible. Some experts say that that playgrounds have become so sterile and boring that kids just walk away from them, preferring instead to hang out in the weeds by the railroad tracks or **throw bottles** in the alley behind the pizza place. Children could actually be placed in more danger by these lame plastic netherworlds that encourage more video game time instead of fresh air and bruising. Another blow to childhood struck by overprotective parents and pesky lawsuits.

Well, we can't change the world, so let's just enjoy the good news: Old, fun, dangerous playgrounds are not completely extinct. Yes, the Safety Conglomerate hasn't killed all the buzz with their rocking horses two inches off the ground, pillowy-soft imitation sand, and **stationary, bolted-on steering wheels**. Old, dangerous playground equipment can still be found. It's out there.

So please, when you find monkey bars taunting you from ten feet off the ground, extended **seesaws** that allow for maximum elevation, and rickety, sagging rope bridges with planks missing, run around like crazy, bump your head a few times, and twist your ankle. Because tell me something—is there anything quite like it?

AWESOME!

Intergenerational dancing

....

Have you ever felt too old or too young on the dance floor?

Maybe you and your husband signed up for a Saturday morning **ballroom dancing class** and noticed everyone else arriving on a shuttle bus from the old folks' home. Or maybe you surprised your wife with a romantic date night on your tenth wedding anniversary and accidentally stumbled into a local college hotspot full of **white baseball caps**, bead necklaces, and Jell-O shooters. Or maybe you just found out the hard way that All-Ages usually means All-Underagers.

I mean, if you've ever found yourself saying "Man, I feel old here," or **"Does anyone else smell Ben-Gay?"** then you know what I'm talking about. It's not that people of different age groups don't socialize, it's just that they don't often groove to the same beats is all.

I think that's why wedding dance floors are a real sight.

They're a breeding ground for that amazing intergenerational dancing that's just so rare and beautiful to see.

You've got grandmas slow-dancing with their **five-year-old grandchildren** to "What a Wonderful World," old men crowd-surfing over a pack of sweaty teenagers, snaking conga lines of all shapes and sizes, and circles forming around anyone who happens to be doing something interesting—

whether that's a father-and-daughter team waltzing in circles or a slightly inebriated bridesmaid **shaking her booty** with a ninety-year-old great-grandpa in a wheelchair.

Yes, intergenerational dancing is a rare and wonderful thing. It's a magical moment where boundaries are broken and the thumping **power of music** sort of sweeps us all together into a tiny little place where everything's just cast aside in favor of living for the moment.

AWESOME!

Flavor pockets

....

Brother, I've made a lot of macaroni.

Yes, for a four-year period back in college I became a regular kitchen whiz at cracking open that flimsy cardboard box of **thin, rock-hard noodles**, boiling them up to a perfect al dente, and stirring in that magical ratio of milk, butter, and pre-packed cheesy powder to get it jussssssssst right.

Now, everyone has their own slightly-altered recipe for boxed macaroni. Some like it thin and milky while others prefer it **bright, radioactive orange**. Some like butter, some margarine, and some toss in a handful of chopped up weenies.

However, no matter how you whip up your noodly batch, I'm guessing you love biting into a surprise flavor patch of undissolved cheesy powder hidden amongst the creamy deliciousness. Yes, every time I scarf down a bowl, no matter how much stirring I've done, there's always that deliciously hidden flavor pocket waiting for me like an old friend.

Yes, **flavor pockets are those delicious sweet spots in the middle of your meal** that explode like surprising fireworks finales in your mouth.

If you're with me here, then come on, let's go nuts and count down five of the finest:

5. **The fat glob of guacamole hiding in your burrito.** When you're sitting in the cramped corner of a dusty Mexican joint, slowly peeling the tin foil off your burrito, chomping at blackened chicken chunks, lime-seasoned rice, and salty pinto beans, it's an amazing feeling when you unearth a treasure trove of chunky guacamole from the dark, inner folds at the back. Note that this also applies to surprise sour cream squirts.

4. **That one bright red chip coated in seasoning.** Clearly the factory foreman at the Dorito Plant fell asleep at his station and accidentally kicked an industrial-sized tin of zesty bold barbecue onto the assembly line. Sure, materials costs shot up, the line was shut down for maintenance, and several union grievances were filed, but it all ended with you savoring a deliciously bright red, salty and super-satured chip.

3. **The spoonful of ice cream with the giant cookie dough chunk.** Fancy ice cream is a frozen clump with swirling lumps of caramel ribbons, candy-coated pralines, and marshmallow globs. Yes, all those wacky tastes are stuck in there like Hans Solo in a

slab of carbonite and it's up to you, the Luke Skywalker of the bench in front of 7-Eleven, to grit your teeth, furrow your brow, and get digging to help them break free of their frozen shackles.

2. **That one lettuce leaf completely drenched in Caesar dressing.** Mmmm, girl. The best part about sliding a creamy leaf of Romaine down your throat is that the leafy green actually gets rid of some of the guilt. "I think this is what the doctor had in mind," you say to your friends, while thick Caesar dressing drips down your chin onto the tablecloth. "High in fiber!" (Note: This also works while eating collared greens soaking in bacon broth or broccoli florets drowning in a giant lake of Cheez Whiz.)

1. **The clump of brown sugar in anything home-baked.** This rare find gets top spot. Sometimes there's a secret glob of pure brown sugar in the peanut butter cookie, oatmeal muffin, or slice of banana bread at Grandma's house. Remember: not even the oven could prevent this sugary jewel from succeeding in its lifelong quest to tantalize your tastebuds.

Yes, flavor pockets are a nice little highlight in the middle of your meal. When those random bites surprise and delight, just close your eyes, tip your head, and savor every single molecule of flavor coating all the cracks and corners of your mouth.

So come on and let's give cracking high fives and throat-screeching cheers for these magic little moments of pure joy.

AWESOME!

Seeing a cop on the side of the road and realizing you're going the speed limit anyway

Stress level goes up.

Stress level goes down.

AWESOME!

Illegal naps

You know what's even better than lying on a hammock in the backyard on a sunny Saturday afternoon? Better than catching a few winks after classes before a long night out at the bars? Better than falling asleep on the couch with the baseball game on the radio? You know what's even better than all that?

I'll tell you what: **illegal naps**, my friend. Sneaking them in when you ain't supposed to.

Napping any time you know you shouldn't be napping has a bit of an edgy, dangerous feel to it, like sneaking into a movie, sharing a free-refill soda at a family restaurant, or coming through customs without declaring the new sweater you're wearing.

I'm talking about driving away from work at lunchtime, parking in a nearby parking lot, tilting back your driver's seat, and sneaking in a little siesta before an afternoon full of meetings. I'm talking about waking up groggily at 11 a.m. after a long night, chomping on handfuls of cold popcorn while surfing the Internet for an hour, then going back to the bedroom to crash all afternoon, building toward that exotic and sinful **Day o' Naps**. Yes, I'm talking about the naps you pull off in the bathroom stall at work, the ones at the back of the bus just before your stop, and the naps you take in the middle of a big bout of procrastination before a deadline, when you convince yourself that a quick snooze will give you more energy to finish that big paper due in a few hours.

So come on! If you're with me, then you agree **life's just too short not to sleep when you feel like it**. So lower those blinds, unplug that alarm clock, and nap strong, nap long, and nap proud, my friends.

AWESOME!

When you get the milk-to-cereal ratio just right

....

Things could go a few different ways near the bottom of that cereal bowl:

1. **Drowning in white.** You poured too fast and over-filled the bowl. Now after you spoon up the soggy O's, you're left with an inch of **sloshy, super-saturated, sandy-colored syrup** at the bottom. Well, the damage is done, so I say bottoms up to that. Just tilt your head, tilt your bowl, and say hello to a peppy morning full of jitters and fast talking.

2. **Cornflake beach.** Here's where you end up with too much cereal and not enough milk. You first notice it when you're halfway through your bowl and those flakes seem **a bit too crunchy for their own good**. So you look down and notice you're swimming in the wading pool, my friend. Assuming you're out of milk **or are very lazy**, you have to frantically start rationing, aiming for just enough milk in each spoonful to get by. Let's hope you make it and don't end up with a fat lump of slightly damp

cornflakes sitting pathetically on the side of your bowl.

3. **Cereal Bowl Bliss.** Oh mama, this here's the perfect milk-to-cereal jackpot. Maybe you're like my friend Mu, who has lifted the art of obtaining **Cereal Bowl Bliss** into a noble, decades-long search for perfection. He has studied milk absorption for years and knows that a bowl of Froot Loops and a bowl of Frosted Flakes have nothing in common other than a mascot who lives in the jungle. See, Mu points out that those Froot Loops float high and dry while Frosted Flakes are like crispy sponges that require a lot more milk to make it through. And then there's the bowl itself. Sure, a big, deep bowl may look great when you pull it out of the cupboard, but watch out for the illusion of size. You may end up drowning in white if you're not careful. Lastly, if you're ready for **Advanced Milking**, you may be interested in the patient art of **The Sit**, which involves letting your beautiful bowl of cereal lie on the counter for a good minute or two before eating. This allows your cereal to soak up a consistent amount of milk and prevents those dreaded bone-dry **first bites of crunchiness** that offset your whole ratio. Remember: This is Advanced Milking, folks. Not for the faint of heart or the extremely hungry.

Anyway, when you get the milk-and-cereal ratio just right at breakfast, you're all aces, my friend. And when you hit it, you hit it, and **you know you hit it**, because that last spoonful goes down smooth without a hint of drowning in white or surfing up onto cornflake beach.

Mm-mm-mm-mm-mmmmmm.

AWESOME!

High-fiving babies

Because they don't usually leave you hanging.
AWESOME!

When you're awkwardly standing by yourself with a full cafeteria tray of food and then suddenly spot your friend waving at you

The dreaded Cafeteria Standalone.

Blue plastic tray wobbling in both hands, carrying a big rolling glass of iced tea and a heavy ceramic plate loaded with steaming roast beef, wet mashed potatoes, and **bland baby carrots**, you exit the cafeteria line and glance at the full crowd in front of you.

It's the high school cafeteria, the workplace lunchroom, or the food court at the mall. Everybody is laughing, **at you maybe**, while you stand and stare out at the kaleidoscopic sea of smiling faces.

As the seconds tick by you feel more and more out of place.

Maybe you quickly glance around the room while **pretending to get ketchup**. Maybe you walk in a couple different directions so you aren't clogging up the lanes or looking too obvious. Or maybe you just get really anxious and wonder if you're going to have to sit by yourself.

But just as you're beginning to lose hope you eventually see them.

It's your friends in the distance.

And they're waving.

AWESOME!

Having a whole row to yourself on the plane

....

It was like a mirage.

There I was a few years ago, sitting in the middle seat of a plane set for take-off, an **empty aisle seat** to my right. I was belted in and cramped, and it just sat there vacant, while overhead bins were slamming shut, flight attendants were bringing out blankets, and passengers started thumbing mindlessly through in-flight magazine articles about **exotic hotel lobbies**.

The plane looked full, the plane looked settled, so I quickly made my **stealth ninjalike swap** into the empty seat like a champion. I moved and sat there with a big smile, lots of elbow room, and my legs comfortably extended into the aisle.

Truly, it was heaven.

Then suddenly a big guy in a **tight business suit** lumbered down the aisle just heaving, sweat dripping down his forehead, tongue wagging out of his mouth like a dog, eyeing my row from a distance. I knew the jig was up, so I moved back to the middle seat as he settled in. Turns out he **slept through his alarm** and had to race to the airport. Nope, no time for a shower, just a full day's worth of grease on his

glistening neck. I voluntarily sacrificed the armrest when his forehead began dripping on me and then tried to enter a cocoon-like state of flying hibernation, covering myself in a blanket, crossing my arms and legs, and trying to go to sleep.

And that's sort of how most plane rides go for me.

But every so often, every once in a while, I'll end up on a pretty empty plane and score an **entire row to myself**. And that's when the perks start piling up. You know how it is:

- **Pee freely.** Yup, get up and go whenever you like, because you won't need to awkwardly limbo past anyone's drink tray. Bonus: no awkward crotch-in-the-face moments.

- **Window and aisle.** It's great looking out the window, but unfortunately the person sitting closest generally gets all window-shade rights. They may close the window completely or block the view when you want a peek. When you get your own row though, you get both.

- **Rest your arms.** All armrests become yours for the taking. Left arm, right arm, it doesn't matter. There's no need to worry about getting the bump-off.

- **Go sideways.** This isn't always easy, but you might be able to pull off the **row nap**, where you flip up all the armrests and turn three seats into a bed.

Forget those pricey lie-down seats in first class—
this here's the Econorest and it works just as well.

Yes, having a whole row to yourself on the plane is a
pretty sweet deal. You can almost pretend that you're **mag-
nificently rich** and paid for the other seats just to buy yourself
some breathing room. Because let's be honest: Flying ain't
always a lot of fun and that extra elbow room can make the
difference between **three hours of misery** and three hours of
bliss.

And that's something worth celebrating.

AWESOME!

Popping Bubble Wrap

Okay, trivia time.

What were the two inventors of Bubble Wrap **trying to make instead of packaging material** back in 1957 at the Sealed Air Corporation? Take a guess and let's see what you got before we reveal the answer in a just a jiffy.

For the patient folks, let's chat for a moment about different ways to do the deed:

1. **Olde Time Classic.** Your average pop. Just squeezing it in your hands with a satisfied smile on your face. Nothing flashy here, folks. Just a thumb, some fingers, and lots of satisfying pops.
2. **The Big Bang.** A trickier move, this one requires delicately wrapping the unpopped Bubble Wrap into a tight ball and then hugging the whole thing against your body really hard. Do this before 10 p.m. so you don't wake the neighbors.
3. **Walk This Way.** You'll need a large piece of Bubble Wrap for this one, likely from a new TV or fridge that got delivered to your house. Just pull the wrap out, lay it down on the floor, take off your socks, and . . . walk all over it. Walk back and forth, walk

in circles, just don't stop the walking, because you can't stop the popping. When the pops slow down, you may have to inspect the wrap closely for any leftover bubbles and take care of those one by one.

4. **The Office Pop.** Here's where you lay it down on the floor of your cubicle and roll over it with your office chair all afternoon. Believe me, your coworkers will love it.

5. **The Twister.** Roll it up like a carpet and twist your hands in opposite directions really hard. When you're done, you'll have a nice well-popped area in the center of your wrap and will have to move on to a new section.

6. **Mini-Pops.** Sometimes you expect to pull out a big, fat mess of Bubble Wrap and out comes a thin, little sheet of mini-bubbles instead. But sometimes that's all you get, man. So do a few mini-pops and enjoy it.

My friends, loudly popping Bubble Wrap is a great joy in life. It's a satisfying stress reliever, a fun surprise, and a rare little moment to **act like a kid** during a boring day at the office or while unpacking after a hectic move.

So, aren't you glad they made Bubble Wrap into packing material and not **textured wallpaper** instead?

AWESOME!

Being the first table to get called up for the dinner buffet at a wedding

....

Weddings can go one of two ways.

Either you're tight like twins with the bride or groom—a sibling maybe, college roommate, or grandmother. You're on **The Inside**, recommending photographers, hosting showers, renting tuxes, giving toasts. For you, the wedding is a great day, a proud moment, a chance to recognize and celebrate someone you love dearly.

Or . . . you're on **The Outside**. You're the groom's doctor, the bride's new boss, or worst of all, the **cousin-date**. You're only there because it would have been rude not to invite you, so you RSVP past the deadline, squeeze into dress clothes from prom, and drink before the reception. You sit at the back table with a lot of people you don't know and introduce yourself to at least one half of the newly married couple late at night on the dance floor during a sweaty party song. "You look really great," you scream over the thumping beats, a nearly full beer swinging wildly in your hand. "I'm Cory, by the way! I work with Linda!"

If you're on The Inside, the entire wedding is wonderful. You cry during speeches, take two hundred pictures, and dance until the lights come up, your hair sweat-glued to your forehead, **big toes** popping through fresh holes in your nylons at two in the morning.

If you're on The Outside, you're scoping out bridesmaids, eating other people's wedding-favor chocolates, and ordering off the menu at the bar.

When you're on The Outside, **there is no greater wedding high than being the first table called up to the dinner buffet.**

Suddenly you're on The Inside, honorary winner of the prestigious Gets to Eat Before Everyone Else Award, dipping your ladle into **Alfredo sauce** before it films over, toothpicking meatballs before they congeal into sugary meat pyramids, and surgically removing the perfect first triangle of cheesecake before the dish gets gummed up with clumpy graham cracker paste and sticky cherry glue.

It sure is a great feeling getting first dibs on that long table of piping hot stream trays. After all, it means you don't have to watch everybody else casually walk by you with full plates while you salivate and attempt to make small talk about where everybody is from and **how beautiful the centerpieces look.**

Yes, if you're up first you walk back to your table a newly crowned king, sitting down at your chair-facing-the-bathroom-at-Table-57 throne, lord and ruler of your much-too-loaded plate of rolled-up salami, potato salad, and gherkins.

AWESOME!

When someone lands on the hotel you just built in Monopoly

....

Shelling out for that primo real estate on the corner lot ain't always easy.

Yes, you may have to mortgage **Electric Company** or dip into that **stash of hundreds** hidden under the game board. But after you make your big investment, there's nothing finer than somebody landing right plum on it, right plum on their next turn.

And there's always a new bit of tension on that first roll after a hotel enters the game too. No more superquick circling and buying properties, collecting **Get Out of Jail** cards, and winning second place in beauty contests. No, now there's a hotel on the board and you enter **Round 2** of Monopoly, where the haves and have-nots are quickly and ruthlessly divided.

When someone lands on the hotel you just built, the first thing they do is get real quiet and quickly pass the dice to the next player, sort of hoping you don't notice that they're squatting on your joint.

But you notice all right.

And maybe you're even all polite and nonchalant about it too.

"Oh, Marvin Gardens? Hold on a second, wait. Yeah sorry, uh, let's see here. That'll be $1,200, please."

"What, seriously?"

"Yeah, sorry. It's the hotel that does it." *(passing the property card over for inspection)*

(inspecting property card) "That's crazy. That's like all my money. I might have to mortgage Baltic Avenue."

"I'm sorry, man. I'll take all the railroads instead if you want."

(disgusted) "What, no way! Then I'll just have Baltic and the blues. Forget it! That's crazy!"

"Fine . . . $1,200, please."

(angrily and slowly counting out and handing you a thick stack of hundreds, twenties, tens, fives, and ones that barely add up to $1,200, leaving them with only a few properties and two ten-dollar bills)

AWESOME!

Finding a mix tape given to you by an old boyfriend or girlfriend

....

Stashed away in **shoe boxes**, basements, and broom closets around the world are some of our greatest treasures.

That's where we might find **old prom photos**, expired driver's licenses, handwritten letters from faraway friends, or maybe, if we're really lucky, one of those beautiful gems known as a **Love Tape**.

Love Tapes are simply any mix tape carefully put together by **someone who *like*-likes you**. Yes, that blurry, distant boyfriend or girlfriend probably spent hours timing everything to fit perfectly, waiting for songs to play on the radio, painstakingly scrawling out notes and drawings, and maybe, if you're lucky, **even spraying it with a bit of perfume.**

Depending on your time frame, your mix tape may contain gems such as:

1. The Righteous Brothers—Unchained Melody
2. Extreme—More Than Words
3. Bryan Adams—(Everything I Do) I Do It for You
4. UB40—(I Can't Help) Falling in Love with You
5. Whitney Houston—I Will Always Love You

6. Meatloaf—I'd Do Anything for Love (But I Won't Do That)
7. Céline Dion—My Heart Will Go On
8. Bob Marley—Is This Love
9. Boyz II Men—End of the Road
10. Jewel—You Were Meant for Me
11. Green Day—Good Riddance (Time of Your Life)
12. Cyndi Lauper—Time After Time
13. The Bangles—Eternal Flame
14. Rod Stewart—Have I Told You Lately
15. LeAnn Rimes—How Do I Live
16. Bon Jovi—Bed of Roses
17. Guns N' Roses—November Rain
18. Milli Vanilli—Girl You Know It's True
19. Sinéad O'Connor—Nothing Compares 2 U
20. Mr. Big—To Be with You

So search your heart. Search your soul. And when you find mix tapes there, you will search no more. So don't tell me they're not worth looking for. You can't tell me they're not worth hunting for. You know it's true.

Everything mix tapes do.

They do it for you.

AWESOME!

Picking the perfect nacho off someone else's plate

....

No two nachos were created equal.

When somebody offers you a nacho from their appetizer plate at a restaurant or while on the couch at home in front of a movie, you need to move fast:

1. First up, quickly scan their entire plate. At what stage is this offer being made? Are you in the game when the plate is hot and full, or are we dealing with mostly crumbs and surplus jalapenos at this point? Size up the prize and give a quick yes or no.

2. Now if you're going in, don't wait too long to make your move. If it's obvious you're putting too much thought into it, you'll come across as selfish. Definitely don't move any toppings around to build yourself a massive **All-In Salad Nacho**, but there's no need to pull out that bland, naked chip at the bottom of the Jenga stack either. You weren't offered crumbs and you don't deserve crumbs. Remember that.

3. Next up, locate your prey and dive in. Everyone has their personal preferences, though I'm a big fan of 90–100 percent melted cheese coverage and about 25–50 percent salsa coverage. Any less cheese coverage and it's just taco shell to me. Any more salsa coverage and I feel like I'm drinking the stuff. And hey, if I grab an olive, green onion, or jalapeno, that's great too, but I don't push my luck. **Lastly, for my money, you can keep that shredded lettuce.** That's just grated water in my book.

Bottom line: Know your tastes, size up the game, and dig in quickly. Mastering that perfect pick is a valuable life skill.

Now go grab life by the nachos.

AWESOME!

The moment at a concert after the lights go out and before the band comes onstage

....

You go early, you grab a drink, you **buy a T-shirt**, you find your seat or you edge up to the stage, you listen to the opening act, you people watch, you watch watch, you talk to your friends, you guess what songs they might play, and then the moment finally arrives: The background music fades down, **all the lights suddenly go out**, and there's total blackness.

You feel a massive wave of anticipation sweep across the crowd, people stand up, raise their arms and scream, and everyone clamors for that first view of the band walking onstage.

AWESOME!

Finding out your birthday is on a Friday or Saturday next year

....

Planning those Wednesday birthdays is tough.

Do you **party-back** on the weekend before or **party-forward** to the weekend after? Either way, you'll get a lot of "So wait, when's your actual birthday?" questions, and you'll be forced to take a sip of your drink, smile pleasantly, and casually say, "Oh, just a couple days from now," or worse, "Oh, you know . . . two Wednesdays ago."

That's just no fun.

So if you're as **self-centered as I am** and the first thing you do when you get your greasy paws on a crisp, new calendar is flip right to your birthday, then you sure are loving it when that big day hits the **Friday or Saturday Jackpot**. Now it's on for so many reasons:

- **Save the date.** No need to puzzle over when to throw the big bash. Just start planning it for that Friday or Saturday. You have no choice and no need to waffle.
- **Party priority.** It's true. When it's your *actual birthday*, your event moves way up the party priority

list. Sure, you're still slightly below Friend's Wedding or Out-of-Town Guest, but you zoom up way higher than Poker Night or Sports Team Banquet.

- **More free drinks.** Especially if you have a birthday party that starts the night before and kicks into high gear at midnight when you **officially** start celebrating. Hopefully you don't have to wear a tiara and a sash to keep those free shots coming.

Yes, you know as well as I do that when that big day lands right on a Friday or Saturday, it opens up a world of celebration possibilities. Because now your birthday's going on, **your birthday's going long**, and your birthday's going strong, fool.

Awwwwwww, yeah.

AWESOME!

Fixing electronics
by smacking them

My room was above the kitchen growing up.

Late at night, lying in bed, I would listen to the creaks and cracks through the vents and floorboards. Oven burners wobbled and popped, distant thumps echoed from the **furnace room**, and the fridge cranked its whirring motor on and off whenever it pleased.

It was always funny to me that during the day the fridge didn't put up much of a fight. If it started clinking and whirring, you just pounded it with your fist and it would stop. One hard **punch to the kidneys** of the thing and it just sort of whimpered and stayed quiet.

Like The Fonz kicking the jukebox on *Happy Days*, Grandpa smacking the TV during *Wheel of Fortune*, or a bandana-clad mom shaking the washer when the heavy towel load gets it rocking, there is something great about fixing electronics by smacking them.

I mean, for once **our instincts work**. That doesn't always happen in nature. Slap a bear on the snout when it's picking through your trash and you might get a friendly mauling. Pull your brother's hair when he steals your Xbox controller and you could find your toothbrush tossed in the toilet. But when the CD is skipping in the car, a friendly smack might do the trick, so how about that?

Also, it kind of **makes you feel handy**. I don't know about you, but I don't know much about electronics. I have no understanding of how telephones work, how airplanes take off, or how radio signals go about their day. I have trouble putting the chain back on my bicycle, **resetting the microwave clock**, or starting the barbecue. You should see me out there, turning the gas on and off, tossing in matches and jumping away, half-expecting the whole thing to blow up.

But I'm not bad at smacking things. I can smack a computer, I can smack a dishwasher, and I've got a lot of experience if your fridge seems to be giving you trouble. So, if you're with me on this one, throw your hand up for a smacking high five and give cheers to your inner handyman.

AWESOME!

Hitting a bunch of green lights in a row

I used to drive home from my friend Mike's basement apartment on this lonely **two-lane road**. It was always late at night and I'd roll down the windows so that the cold country-time air could help keep me awake. The air smelled like a cologne **Beetlejuice** might wear—a tangy combination of fresh manure, foggy dew, and **squashed skunk**.

Yes, I'd say it was a nice, quiet way to end an evening, a relaxing and peaceful drive home on those late nights.

But then they came.

The big-box stores gobbled up that cheap farmer land and dropped in a **concrete paradise** full of parking lots, neon signs, and a never-ending series of traffic lights that completely clogged up the roads. The cold farm air was replaced by a new smell, a thick, heady mix of car exhaust and fried chicken.

And, you know, I understand.

Every massive parking lot really does need its own traffic light. I mean, without them, you'd be stuck trying to make a left turn out of **Home Depot** for half an hour. You buy those two-by-fours, you want to go build that deck, am I right? No really, I get it. I've been there too, and I get the lights.

But let's be honest: **The resulting gauntlet** is no good either.

On that old drive home from Mike's basement apartment they built up more than ten traffic lights in a row, each only about a couple hundred feet apart. There was traffic light after traffic light after traffic light, a sort of slow death march through the **jungle of progress**.

And the lights never lined up. You'd hit two greens, then two reds. You'd race through a couple of last-second yellows and then get your comeuppance with five reds in a row. Yes, it was a frustratingly, fuel-wastingly, **stop-and-go-to-slow** ordeal.

Now, one night I was driving home from Mike's place a little later than usual. We started a movie when we should've called it a night, and I was trucking home at **three in the morning on a Tuesday**. I approached The Gauntlet groggily and hit the first few green lights in a row, no problem. Nothing special, I figured, probably just a tease. After all, **The Gauntlet had never lost**.

But then, before I knew it, I had made a couple more.

Then a couple more.

Then a couple more.

Suddenly I was two lights away from the finish line and I couldn't believe my luck. Looking ahead I could see that both lights were green, tempting me, showing me what might be possible.

So I gunned it.

I blew through the second-to-last green and saw that final one turn to yellow. There was no way I was going to get that close without making it through, so I punched the gas and barely squeezed by as the light turned red.

Although almost running a red wasn't the smartest move in the book, making it through The Gauntlet was one of the greatest accomplishments of my life. I was **buzzing huge** that night and smiling ear to ear. And really, just tell me the truth—if you've ever blown through a string of green lights in a row, how does it make you feel?

I've got just one guess.

AWESOME!

When you push the button for the elevator and it's already there

Ding!

AWESOME!

Bakery air

Bakery air is that **steaming hot front** of thick, buttery fumes waiting for you just inside the door of a bakery. And I am just going to tell you straight up: **That is some fine air.**

Bakery air immediately fills you up with the sickly sweet smell of rising cupcakes, **crisping croissants**, and the distinct aroma of globby oatmeal turning into a delicious tray of sugary-brown cookies.

It's a powerful and intoxicating smell that rivals some of the best smells out there: late night summer barbecue, new car smell, gasoline, fresh baby, or even, dare I say it, campfire in the woods. Yes, I went there.

Now, is it just me, or do you ever feel sorry for the people working in the bakery? You know, because they might just **get used to the smell** and stop enjoying those hot bakery whiffs all the time? I really hope it's not like that. I really hope working in a bakery never turns into a regular job full of early mornings, **oven-scorched eyebrows**, varicose veins, and floury underwear. No, bakery air is just too good for that. It can't become another day at the office, it just can't. So let's make sure we all enjoy it.

Catch some of those sugary vapors next time you're running past a **cinnamon bun** place at the train station. Suck back a noseful of hot fumes when you walk the dog by an open bakery door on Saturday morning. And make sure when you stop to smell the roses, you stop to smell the croissants and cookies too.

AWESOME!

Tripping and realizing no one saw you

....

Babies take a while to walk.

If you've seen it happen, you know there is plenty of falling, crawling, and bawling. Hey, there's a reason most two-year-olds are covered in fat lips, skinned knees, and **coffee-table-dented foreheads**.

Learning to walk ain't easy.

Sure, you did it and I did it but we probably couldn't do it again. Like learning anything tough and life-altering, learning to walk is a **messy process** that takes time and patience.

First, there is rolling. That cute little **baby-powder ball** of flabby arms and puffy nappies twists and shimmies on the cold linoleum with a big smile on her face. This marks a major step as baby is learning to move on her own. Don't laugh because you were once a flabby, wiggling nappy ball too.

Once that's nailed, it's time to **sit up** and **start crawling**. This turns the house into a carpeted jungle full of discovery and adventure. Curiosity helps little ones discover pantry shelves, cat litter trays, and toilets. Some people have an adorable **Crab Baby** at this stage, also known as a one-year-old who crawls backward or sideways instead of forward. Watch out for pinchy claws grabbing at your hair and glasses.

Next up: **teetering!** White-knuckled, apricot-sized hands grip staircase railings and kitchen table legs with furrowed brows and steely determination. The side benefit of nappies comes into play here, as handy ass-padding for the vast number of harrowing, thunderous falls. Eventually, with immense focus and concentration, most of them manage to find their center of gravity and balance the baby chub on their two teeny-tiny tootsies.

After this point, it's just a matter of time. There's some nervous balancing without the railing and then lopsided running with occasional face-plants in the front hallway. But soon baby nails it, and after that she's probably flying pretty high.

Unfortunately, the bad news is that practice doesn't always make perfect. Even though we've been mastering the art of standing tall for years and years and years, everyone slips and falls now and then. Just ask your local small-claims court.

So next time your shoe catches on the top step at work, you trip stepping off the airport's **moving sidewalk**, or you bail on a patch of ice outside your front door, remember that not too long ago you couldn't walk at all.

So your wipeout is really no big deal.

As long as nobody saw you.

AWESOME!

The Universal Fry-Sharing Policy

The Universal Fry-Sharing Policy states that if you are eating a meal with someone who ordered fries, and you didn't order fries, you're entitled to grab one of their fries as it's landing on the table as long as a) you ask first, b) you make eye contact and raise your eyebrows until they nod, or c) you just know them really well.

Also, since you're getting first dibs on their **sizzling stick-pile** of delicious hot, oily fries, it's only fair that you purposefully avoid any **obviously amazing fry** in the pile. You know that really, really long McDonald's fry sticking out of the box? Probably shouldn't touch that. But the thin, crispy short ones, the oversalted ones, and the regular **limp 'n' floppy** ones? Those are all fair game, my friend, all fair game.

But be careful out there because this policy can be abused. Some people might start pecking away at the fry-pile, then just start gaining momentum, **unable to stop gorging** themselves on your plate once they get started. They just keep testing the waters, pushing the envelope, snacking away until you move your plate out of reach or ask them politely how their food tastes. I'm serious—you need to watch out for these people because they'll dent your fry-pile if you're not careful.

Secondly, keep your eyes peeled for greasy diner plates that come with only **a dozen or so baked-potato-tasting fries**. You know what I'm talking about. Those piles are off-limits! Sorry, but the Universal Fry-Sharing Policy simply does not cover extremely small piles of chunky-style fries. It would be too much to take one of those fries. The percentages just don't work.

Finally, there is **one appendix** to The Universal Fry-Sharing Policy. Conveniently it is called **Appendix One**, and it simply states that after somebody who ordered fries finishes their meal and pushes their leftover pile of dry, cold, ketchup-smeared fries into the center of the table, **first dibs go to people who didn't get fries**. Second dibs go to those who already de-molished a stack of them but just want more. And third dibs go to the guy washing dishes in the kitchen.

So thanks, Universal Fry-Sharing Policy. Your existence is a **win-win**, balancing the tables by helping us fry guys trim down the calories and helping the "Can I sub salad for fries?" folks enjoy some guilty pleasure while still meeting their **eatin' healthy** goals.

AWESOME!

Sleeping in new bedsheets

You know the feeling: You just spent five minutes chasing all the corners of the elastic form-fitting bottom sheet around your bed and then laid and **tucked the top sheet tightly into the mattress**. You found some pillow covers in the linen closet, squeezed and shook your pillows in there, put your blanket over all of it, took a deep breath, and then dove right into the fresh, cold, mothball-smelling sheets.

New sheets are great because they don't smell like **The Sleeping You**, with your armpit hair all squishing around in there all night, your drool leaking all over the pillows, and your crusty old feet flaking off into little piles of dead skin shavings at the foot of the bed. And let's not forget the hot farts you pop out when you're sleeping too. Don't deny it! We're all disgusting when we're asleep, and new bed sheets are great for letting us temporarily escape our own filth.

Really, only one thing can add to that new bedsheet feeling and that's when it's your **first seasonal sleep** in thin cotton summer sheets or thick linen winter sheets. As you close your eyes softly, crickets chirping outside your window, moonlight and tree branches shadowdancing on the walls, you know right then and there: It's going to be a good night.

AWESOME!

Using hotel lobby bathrooms when you're out walking around

···

Anyone else out there have a bladder the size of a walnut? One that fills up after a few spoons of soup and is at attention, ready to drain any time of the day? If you're afraid of getting a drink before the movie or having a glass of water anytime after 6 p.m., then you're with me. My small and weak-bladdered brothers and sisters of the world, unite!

See, we got issues, me and you. We're terrible on airplanes. We never get to experience the 7-Eleven Super Big Gulp. And maybe worst of all, **we're always forcing our friends to help us find public washrooms** when we're walking or driving anywhere, which really drives them crazy. Sorry, friends.

If you're with me on this one, then you know these searches for decent public washrooms really are a fine art. Those perfect places are always out there, but you really need to be careful. With that warning let's discuss the **Top Five Places to Pee When You're Out:**

5. **Gas stations.** Easy prey for the worst kind of fly-by urinators—those who don't live nearby or plan on

coming back. These people do not respect bathroom facilities. We know this from racist scrawls on bathroom walls and the mistaking of floors for toilets. Bad ones smell rancid. Good ones smell like a flatbed truck full of urinal pucks sitting on a garbage dump. But hey, sometimes they appear like mirages on the horizon, and at least you know they're almost always open and have a toilet. So we give you Number 5, gas stations. Thanks for coming out.

4. **Bus or train stations.** Bus or train station bathrooms are just like gas stations but with one major difference: maintenance. Whereas gas stations are run by individual owner-operators or a couple of teenagers working the midnight shift, bus or train stations are generally run by formal transit authorities or governments who employ people **just to clean the place up**, because otherwise they'd look bad or get kicked off the board of transportation or something. The other plus to bus or train stations is size. They usually have **rows** of stalls or urinals instead of **one**. Very little chance of having to wait. So thanks, bus or train station bathroom. You're there when we need you.

3. **Restaurants or coffee shops.** Okay, we're starting to get into decent territory now. Maybe an extra ply on the toilet paper or perhaps a comic strip pinned

up over the urinal. Restaurant and coffee shop bathrooms are much better, but they are a little hard to get at—you've either got to buy something or pretend you're looking for someone before running to the back of the place and then taking off. Care and delicacy is required. Not for the faint of heart.

2. **Somebody's nearby house.** This is where you make the mid-trip pit stop at a local friend's apartment or house. They don't necessarily have to be hanging out with you at the time. Just buzzing their place and asking if you can use the facilities is acceptable. And once you get in you'll be living large with thick toilet paper, fancy cream soap, and occasionally a stack of dog-eared magazines. Try not to judge the hair in the sink, bath towel on the floor, or bright, glowing toilet bowl ring staring up at you like the Eye of Sauron. Just enjoy and get out.

1. **Hotel lobby bathrooms.** Now we finally reach the cream of the crop, the cherry on the sundae, the top of the roller coaster. Yes, the spacious, luxurious, over-the-top hotel lobby bathrooms really are magical when you've been walking around all day, sweating under the blazing sun, just searching for somewhere to lighten your load. Hotel lobby bathrooms are great because they are so sinful. Really,

nothing in there is necessary, but you become the **Emperor of Toilets**, commander over a vast plumbing kingdom, ruler of all taps and mirrors for miles around. Hotel lobby bathrooms treat us streetwalkers like uppity business-class travelers. I mean, who likes to dry their hands with face cloths anyway? Who needs chairs in the bathroom? And who really wants one of those bathroom butlers sneakily wedged into a corner wearing a tux and holding out cologne and towels for you? Who needs this?

Well us, that's who! We thimble-bladdered folk need this once in a while. I'm sorry but we need it. A little pampering and comforting for our terrible genetic sins. So thank you, hotel lobby bathrooms for treating us with grace and dignity amongst a world of people who don't like to hang out with us.

AWESOME!

Taking your bra off after wearing it for hours

It just feels like freedom.

Or so I've heard.

AWESOME!

The sound of scissors cutting construction paper

When you hear scissors cutting through a sheet of construction paper, you just know fun is about to happen. The table is covered with glue sticks, glitter, pipe cleaners, and **googly eyes**, and everything is set for a day full of crafts with the camp counselor.

In some ways, this is essentially the kid equivalent of spreading tools out across the **basement workbench** before building a shelf, or taping windows and opening paint cans before you coat the kitchen walls in a new shade.

Yes, the sound of scissors cutting construction paper is the sound of important work about to happen. It's the sound of creativity bubbling. It's the sound of ideas blossoming. And it's the sound of some decent fun on a rainy afternoon.

AWESOME!

Waking up before your alarm clock and realizing you've got lots of sleep time left

....

Dark windows, **dead silence**, dim moonlight dancing on the walls. The night is calm and quiet and peaceful.

And then **BOOM**.

Your eyes burst open and you bust out of bed in an adrenaline-gushing, brain-rushing state of emergency. Dizzy and blind, you **urgently stumble** over to the clock as thoughts zoom through your head—am I late for work, did I miss the buzzer, do I have time for a shower?

You swipe the clock, zoom it up to your **squinty eyeballs**, and get a good look.

"4:56 a.m.," it screams in its trademark bright-red fluorescent silence.

"4:56 a.m."

Your hazy half-asleep brain slowly clicks into gear. "Much early than morning," you piece together slowly. "Time more sleep now."

And then a slow, thin smile curls on your lips as you turn to stare at your **crumpled cocoon** and dive back into **Bedhead Paradise**. Oh, you know that second dip into Dreamland will be a doozy for a few big reasons:

- **Ready to rock.** The bed is pre-warmed, the mattress pre-dented, and the other side of the pillow is just waiting to hug your hot, salty head. Detangle the sheets and you're good to go.
- **Dare to dream.** If that rocking dream you're having is still fresh in your head, you might be able to clench your eyes, squeeze your brain, and pop right back into it.
- **Take a break.** Your body woke up early because it felt pretty rested, so the extra sleep is just its way of saying "Go ahead, take a long lunch." People, this is like a snow day without the shoveling—just a big puddle of free time to soak up guilt-free.

Yes, waking up before your alarm clock and realizing you've got lots of sleep time left is a great thing. Sure, your heart pulses and your **brain convulses**, but you quickly realize there's a long time to go before morning.

So snore on and snooze strong, my friends.

AWESOME!

When the socks from the dryer all match up perfectly

....

Peeling apart that static-covered **clump of socks** is tense.

First you yank them from the dryer and dump the **hot haystack** on the bed. Then you start pairing up the easy ones—reconnecting brown argyle husbands with brown argyle wives and red-striped brothers with red-striped sisters. It's free and easy love all around.

But then it happens.

You hit that big pile of white or black **leftover socks** and matching gets tough. You're inspecting patterns and heel placements, checking textures and fades, all the while hoping, just hoping, that everything will work out fine.

As you approach the last few socks you do a quick mental count to see if you've got **an even number** of socks left on the bedspread.

If you do, and if they all match up perfectly, then you're loving it. There are no missing **tube socks** or disappearing dress socks. Everything is locked and loaded, so you just put them all together, take that basket of well-worn lovers to the dresser, and dump them all in the drawer with a **big smile** on your face.

AWESOME!

When there's still time left in the parking meter when you pull up

....

Say some kind and generous soul left **seven unused minutes** on the parking meter and left you with three big choices.

First of all, you could go with the **No Dollar Dash**. This is where you do some quick mental math and figure you can run all your errands before the time expires. If you can grab a slice of pizza and pick up the dry cleaning that quickly, then go man, just go.

Then again, maybe No Dollar Dashing is too stressful for you. You're afraid of the parking ticket, so you go instead with the **Tight Quarter Squeeze**. Here's where you plug a warm quarter in there because you're sure seventeen minutes will be good enough. Hey, you're still thankful for the seven free minutes but figure it's worth buying yourself a brisk walk in place of a run.

Lastly, you could go **Slot Machine**. You're one of those folks who just don't trust themselves. The parking ticket must be avoided at all costs, even if it means dumping an extra couple dollars in the meter. You buy yourself a big, warm security blanket in case you get held up somewhere.

And now, even though most of us would like to think of

ourselves as laid-back No Dollar Dash kind of folks, let's be honest. We love the **Slot Machines**, because they're the ones who leave us with seven minutes left the next time. And if it wasn't for the **Tight Quarter Squeezers** and their perfect parking planning, getting seven minutes of free time would just become no big deal.

So by holding hands and joining together, we all make that world go right on round.

AWESOME!

The smell of crayons

Crack open a fresh box and get ready for a neuron-splattering head rush.

AWESOME!

Peeling an orange in one shot

It ain't easy, but when you finally succeed in peeling an orange into only one **big, swirly peel**, it can be one of the greatest fruit-eating experiences of your life. Here's how to make the magic happen:

1. **Pick a winner.** No two oranges are created equal, so it's important to inspect your fruit before you pick it. Smart money says grab a juicy one that's been ripe for a day or two and has plenty of loose, saggy peel hanging around just begging for a big thumb puncture right in the gut. If you have trouble, just remember this handy line: **To get that peel off, pick one that's soft.** Word to your sister.

2. **Roll it out (optional).** Some people like to roll their orange around on the counter a bit just to make doubly sure that the peel is primed and ready to go. This is the equivalent of sending the orange out to the bullpen to warm up. A side benefit is that your orange becomes extra juicy.

3. **The thumb puncture.** This is the most critical move, so let's break it down. First, make sure you do actually use your thumb to perform the puncture,

not the questionable four-fingers-scratching-the-blackboard technique. People who go the four-finger route are doomed to get peel scraps flying everywhere, so don't do it. Now, when you have your game face ready, aim for one of the flabby peel rolls right near the top or bottom of the orange. No matter what, do not stab right in the middle of the fruit, because that's the thinnest part of the peel and you'll walk away a humiliated, pulpy mess.

4. **Long, slow burn.** Once you're in, it's time to slowly, majestically carve out a big peel strip around and around and around the orange. Be careful not to create any **peel islands**, those little chunks of peel just hanging out in the middle of a freshly peeled area. Also, don't peel too thick a strip (inaccurate and unpredictable) and don't peel too thin a strip (could snap off). Just relax and it will come with practice. If you seem to be losing your momentum or getting stressed out, put the orange down, shake your hands out, take some deep breaths, and regroup.

5. **Show and tell.** Did you nail it? Did you finish it off good? If so, congratulations, you're now holding a freshly shorn orange in one hand and a limp 'n' long, snakelike strip of peel in the other. You have

to finish by showing this to at least one person and saying "Hey, check it out!" Maybe hang it right in their face if they don't seem impressed at first. They should come around and at least flash you a terse thumbs-up or a sarcastic eyebrow raise.

Yes, peeling an orange in one shot is a terrific accomplishment. It's one of the best fruit openings out there, easily trumping the watermelon split, **pineapple top lop**, or coconut crack.

AWESOME!

Using all the different shampoos and soaps in someone else's shower

···

Shampoo doesn't travel well.

First of all, you can barely get it on the plane. Nope, **no liquids in your carry-on**, so unless you've got a little travel bottle or you're checking in a big suitcase, you can't really take it. And even if you do check it in, you've got the packing problem. I know my terrible method of putting a big bottle of shampoo in a couple plastic bags isn't the answer. But what is? Travel bottles are more trouble than they're worth— you have to play **sloppy scientist** to refill them and they're small and easy to forget everywhere.

No, shampoo just doesn't travel well. Like fireworks, katana blades, or **colicky babies**, it just wasn't meant to fly. So if you're like me, you just don't pack it. You swallow hard, zip that suitcase, and trust that your hair will make it home.

When you hit the road without shampoo, a few things could happen:

1. You might have to slum it, **oily style**. Just work that comb and pray for no dandruff.

2. You might have to use one of the little hotel bottles of shampoo or tear into one of their tiny little shampoo samples with your teeth in the shower. If you're like me, you'll probably use the lotion in your hair too, thinking it's conditioner.

3. Best-case scenario: You're crashing with friends and you get to **take a shower in their shower** and go wild using all the different shampoos and soaps they've got in there.

Now, we all know the last option is clearly the best. However, it only works if you actually are staying with friends **and** if you shower in their **real shower**—not their guest shower, not their basement shower, but their **actual shower**, the one they use every day. That's where you peel back their crinkly, mildewed curtain and open up a fantasy world of half-used bizarro products filling all corners of the bathtub, piled high in bright pinks and neon greens like a candy store.

So go ahead: Lock that door, strip right down, and get right in there. Just make sure you follow the **Top Four Showering in Other People's Shower Rules**:

1. **Bar Ban.** The bar of soap is completely off-limits, no questions asked. You don't know where it's been, they don't know where you're putting it, so you

just have to stay away. The last thing anyone wants for a thank-you gift is a nest of wet hairs in the soap dish.

2. **Watch the clock.** Definitely enjoy the moment, but don't take too long. You don't know their hot water situation or if they need the bathroom, so get out before you get the place too steamy. And leave the fan on.

3. **Sampling is encouraged.** If you're staying with a couple, chances are good they've got His and Hers sections. Try both! What's this? New scent of body wash? Squirt! Weird kiwi-grapefruit face wash? Squirt! Forty-dollar-a-bottle salon conditioner that looks like it came from a science lab? Squirt squirt squirt!

4. **Don't finish anything.** Squirt away, but don't drain anything. They might be counting on one last use of their favorite conditioner and you don't want to rob them of that.

So that's it. That's the perfect traveling shampoo situation and them's the rules for living by it.

Now, is it just me, or does using all the different shampoos and soaps in someone else's shower make you feel like you're in some kind of **focus group**? You can just see the end of it too: A few folks in white smocks hold clipboards waiting for you outside the bathroom door in the dark hallway. It flies open and steam shoots out in all directions. You emerge in a towel, your skin damp, your feet wet. And quickly, there are questions: "What did you think of the blue bottle? Did it give you the lather you were looking for? What about the scent?" They keep going, writing furiously as you spit out your first impressions. Then they ask the big one: **"What was the shower experience like overall?"** They wait expectantly, heads bowed, pencils hovering just above the sheet, eyes peering up at you over their glasses.

And you smile and you nod and you know what to tell them.

AWESOME!

When the vending machine gives you two things instead of one

First you spot the **Teetering Treat**.

It's the candy bar hanging onto the metal spirals for dear life, just sitting there after giving the last customer the ol' **For Sale Fail** and teasing him instead of delivering the goods. And instead of spending another dollar to test his luck, he decided to walk away. Hey, we've all been there too, so now it's time for some good old-fashioned Vending Machine Karma, also known as **Chocolate Justice**.

So just drop your money in, push the buttons, and listen for that sweet **thump-thump** of two treats dropping into the **Sugar Basin** at once. Now push back the awkwardly heavy door and swipe a paw in there to scoop up your treasures. Kiss the vending machine plastic window, hold your nougat-filled plunder up to the sky, and then flee the scene.

It's snacking time.

Yes, that free treat is great because now's your chance to **play Santa** on an unsuspecting coworker or classmate. Got someone who could use a caramel fix? Of course you do. So share the wealth and give yourself a break together. It's Christmas again.

Also, no matter how much you try, **you can't return the free snack**. No, there's no wedging your hand up there and throwing it back into its Metal Spiral Jail Cell. So ditch the guilt and smile back at the **Gods of Snacking**, for they have smiled down upon you.

And let me tell you something else: You deserve it.

AWESOME!

Licking the batter off the beaters of a cake mixer

....

You can't do it without getting batter all over your face, because there's that hard-to-reach place in the middle of the beater. Your tongue isn't going to reach, and leaving it unlicked isn't an option. So get in there, get sticky, and get

AWESOME!

Being the first person into a really crowded movie theater and getting the prime seats

··

When it comes to movie theater seats, everybody has their favorite.

First up, there's the **Back Row Crowd**. We all know these people because most of us have been these people. With nobody behind you the back row becomes a prime make-out spot, a perfect place to sneak sips from your secret flask, or just somewhere to place your really tall and lanky body without blocking anyone's view. Thanks for that, by the way.

Next you've got your **Middle of the Packers**. These folks go for some of the most popular seats—the middle seats in the middle row about midway back. They might go on about how the sound is better from straight ahead or how they get a headache from sitting too close, but I think they just like being in the thick of things. And who can blame them?

Side Guys, that's who. Yes, the folks who enjoy sitting in the thin side sections of the movie theater are a rare breed, but they're out there. Maybe they have pea-sized bladders or fidgety children in tow and need access to a quick getaway lane. Or perhaps they want some thinking space and don't like fighting for armrests. Whatever their reasons, I think

I can safely say that most of us are glad they exist, because they really help our odds at getting the other seats.

And we can't forget the **La-Z-Boys 'n' Girls**. These are the folks who put their feet up on the seat in front of them. "I came here to relax," they seem to say to themselves. "So I'm going to relax." They have no problem taking up a seat in front of them with their dirty sneakers or corn-covered heels. Brave souls may even try to pull off the **Extreme La-Z-Move**, which involves very slowly and softly putting their feet on the chair in front of them despite someone already sitting in it. It does not involve making new friends, generally. But these folks like their feet up so they'll even take a corner seat that nobody wants to pull it off.

Lastly, there are the **Front Row Crazies**. You know, I used to think people who sat in the front section just had incredibly poor judgment . . . *and incredibly good chiropractor coverage! Hey-ohhhhhhh!* But seriously, craning their necks sky-high, rolling their heads left to right the whole time, what were they thinking? But then I realized that some of these people are just my friend Mike, who always realizes at the last minute that he forgot his glasses and forces us to sit near the front so he can see the screen.

So sure, everybody has **their favorite seat**. The problem is that we don't always get them.

Some people buy tickets online and line up really early, so when we get to the theater they're already there, waiting near the garbage can, **smacking their gum**, reading their free movie magazine. No, we're not going to beat those folks unless we want to play their game. And their game is generally pretty long and tedious.

Other times people seem to know a back route or something. You think you're going to get a good seat, but suddenly there are **two ladies** sitting there out of nowhere, stretching out their sweaters and purses across a long row to save room for all their friends. They're like **nervous hens**, eyeing you suspiciously like you might grab an egg and take off. They get right into it too. I've seen a stretchy wool sweater cover four seats. That's some serious wingspan.

Basically, it's pretty tough to get perfect seats these days. The crowds are big, the crowds are feisty, and the **prime plushes** ain't easy to come by. But isn't that what makes it so special when you really nail it? When you skip up those stairs, eye your prize, toss your windbreaker in front of you, and grab your perfect little bank of seats before the big show? I hope you'll agree that getting those perfect movie seats is like **melted joy** and sizzling happiness served on the big pizza pie of heaven.

Because you won this game, my friend. You came, you sat, and you won.

AWESOME!

The Kids Table

The Kids Table is where all the kids eat dinner at holiday family gatherings.

It's generally a rickety card table from the basement pushed beside a **yellow plastic one** from the playroom that ends up turning Grandma's hallway into an eat-in kitchen. Sometimes it's two different heights, sometimes the chairs are broken, and usually the whole thing is covered in a plastic Christmas tablecloth freshly ripped from the **dollar store** cellophane.

No matter what though, The Kids Table is a great place to find **burps, laughs, and juice spills** at a holiday meal. Everyone's enjoying a warm evening, with cousins decked out in their finest cableknit sweaters, rosy red cheeks, and **massive bedhead**.

Yes, The Kids Table is great for many reasons.

First off, **no parents** means no problems. Nope, they're all baking pies, playing ping-pong, or sipping eggnog by the fireplace. The parenting theory here is that the kids sort of form a **group safety net** that will likely come screaming if somebody gets hurt, so no need for a pesky watchful eye. With all adults distracted, rules fly out the window and suddenly elbows lean up on tables, **chewed-up brussel sprouts** get hidden in napkins, and somebody starts eating mashed pota-toes with their bare hands.

And no matter how old everybody is, the rule at The Kids Table is that you must act like you're seven. Teenagers who think they're too old for the table quickly start blowing bub-bles in their milk, **pouring salt in people's drinks**, and giggling like mad. Then someone pops a **loud fart** and everyone laughs for ten straight minutes.

Lastly, let's not forget that The Kids Table eats first and sometimes features special items like lasagna with no onions, random chopped-up hot-dogs, or real Coke.

People, a lot of good times and great moments happen at The Kids Table. Little ones learn from older siblings and cousins. Childhood bonds and friendships are formed over toys, tears, and **gravy spills**. And for kids, it's good practice for eating with high-school pals at the local greasy spoon when someone gets their driver's license, or scarfing a hungover breakfast with college roommates at the dining hall.

So thank you, The Kids Table.

For all you do.

AWESOME!

The final seconds of untangling a really big knot

I don't know how to tie my shoes.

I know, I know, it's terrible, it's embarrassing, but I seriously can't tie my shoes the way most people do. I just—my fingers don't slide the right way. When I try the loop-around-and-pull-through move, I end up with a **limp and loose** version of the finished product. As a result, I'm stuck with **The Bunny Ears Method**, also known as The Double Loop or Grandma Knot. Yes, I make a loop with my right hand, a loop with my left, and then I tie them together. It's a tiny bit slower, but that's not the worst of it.

The worst of it is that it often results in **massive, tightly wound knots** that take forever to untie.

So basically I try to avoid untying my shoes altogether. Instead, I spend one or two minutes wedging and banging my foot into them each time I leave the house. Although this technique results in completely squashing the back of my shoe, I find it preferable than sorting out the granddaddy knot waiting for me down there.

But sometimes there is no choice.

See, at some point my scraggly knot will lie lazily on the side of my shoe, staring up at me with its sad, dusty face. And

I can only smile wearily, shake my head, sit down on a step, and get ready to slog away in the five-minute heavyweight title card of **Me vs. The Knot.**

I'm not going to lie: I often lose this battle, choosing instead to throw on a pair of sandals or stay home and order pizza. But there are also days where I come out on top. There are days where I stick my fingernail in there as hard as I can and pick and pick and pick until the lace finally starts to give. And then I start pulling it this way and that way until I can finally see **the light at the end of the tunnel**, the moment of truth, the dream becoming a reality.

Those final few seconds of untangling a really big knot happen in a hazy slow motion. A twisted lace becomes loose, and then another, and then there is some frantic untying as it all comes undone.

Yes, whether it's headphone wires, **Nintendo controllers**, phone cables, or Christmas lights, it sure feels great during the last few seconds of untangling that tightly tied mess.

AWESOME!

The Five Second Rule

The Five Second Rule simply states that any **food dropped on the floor** is perfectly fine to eat as long as you pick it up in less than five seconds.

The rule has many variations, including The Three Second Rule, The Seven Second Rule, and the extremely handy and versatile **However Long It Takes Me to Pick Up This Food Rule**. But whatever version you use, there's just no denying why it's great:

1. **Makes you look less disgusting.** Because now when you eat that wet grape that rolled into the corner by the heating vent and collected some cat hair and a few dry toast crumbs, you're not disgusting. No, you're just a law-abiding Kitchen Citizen. Big difference.

2. **Saves time and money.** Wait, wait, wait, don't pull the peanut butter and jelly out again and make a whole new sandwich. No, we'll just blow the floor spice off this one and maybe tear off the wet, soggy piece of crust that landed in the juice puddle. It's all good.

3. **It's scientifically proven.** Well, actually it's scientifically proven that if a floor is covered in salmonella or E. coli, your food will be covered in salmonella or E. coli, even if they touch for only a split second. But, and here's the kicker, that same University of Illinois study showed **no significant evidence of contamination on public flooring** in general. Good save, Science.

So people, I give you a friend and savior in these tough times: The Five Second Rule. Know it. Love it.

Live by it.

AWESOME!

When the thing you were going to buy is already on sale

Advertisers eat me up.

Honestly, whenever I leave the **grocery store** I feel like I've just been had by the lot of them. I fully confess it too. I wheel in for toilet paper and wheel out with a fat cart loaded to the gills with **supersize salsa**, a dozen croissants, and two new brands of frozen pizza.

It hits me like a hammer at the cash register, but by then it's too late.

Yes, I reluctantly pay the bill as my mind flashes back to the **Me of 15 Minutes Ago**, a barely recognizable guy humming down the aisle and happily accepting little sample cups of drinkable yogurt from **sweet old ladies in hairnets** while casually tossing econo-size cheese bricks and vacuum-sealed meat sticks into my shopping cart.

Oh, I'm a happy camper amongst the freshly misted lettuce and bubbling lobster tanks, but when I get to the front and get **cash register slapped** it's a different story.

If you're with me, then you know that's why it so great when you go to the store and **the thing you were going to buy is already on sale**. Suddenly the tables have turned and now you're calling the shots.

"Oh, what's this?" you ask innocently, approaching a towering display of toilet paper on sale for half price. "Half off, really? Well that's perfect because that's all I came here for anyway. And you know what, may as well get **seven extra dozen** while I'm here too."

(looking around the store with raised eyebrows) "Annnnnnnd I guess that's everything for today."

Then you mime making a big check mark on your grocery list and smile as you savor the moment sweetly. Yes, now your wallet stays fat, **your smile stays fresh**, and you ride the fast lane straight to Penny-Pinching Heaven.

AWESOME!

Peeling that thin plastic film off new electronics

Welcome to the world, remote control. We're happy to have you with us, laptop monitor. You're free, cell phone.

AWESOME!

Finding your keys after looking forever

....

Panic sets in very slowly.

It's early in the morning and you're heading out for work. After flicking your lights off and stomping your shoes on, you casually tap your pockets and find them surprisingly dentless.

"No big deal," you think with a mild shrug. "Probably left them on the kitchen counter."

So you swing by the kitchen only to find no dice, man, no dice at all. You double-check your pants, flip through your purse, and pause for a split second to stare at the microwave clock while doing some math. Figuring you need to leave in seven minutes so you're not late for work, you suddenly ditch your jacket on the floor and go perform the classic Key Hunting Play in three acts:

Act 1: The Slow Build. The curtain rises to a scene of you rescanning the kitchen counter, triple-checking your pockets, and then searching the rest of the house in an increasingly frantic panic. You walk all over the carpet as your forehead starts sweating and you begin checking more and more obscure places. Violinists in the pit band work into a frenzy as thunder crashes outside the window, while you check the bathroom counter, desk drawers, and fridge but come up empty.

And it is black.

Act 2: The Detective. The dusty spotlight shakes and stops on a shot of you pausing by the front door. You grimace at the ceiling, sucking in deep breaths, scratching your head. A dog barks faintly in the distance and thunder cracks again as you suddenly transform into a detective, pausing to retrace your steps from where you saw your keys last.

"I came home, I went upstairs, I changed into sweatpants," you recall quietly to the hushed crowd. "I ate a frozen burrito, I checked my email, I fell asleep on the couch . . ."

There is a long, drawn-out pause.

And it is black.

Act 3: The Greatest Hits. Running out of options, your mind flashes back to your greatest hits, a quick-clicking slideshow of places you've found your lost keys in the past. The audience is treated to brilliant back-screen images of happier days. Sporting a lower hairline, flatter stomach, and tighter T-shirt, a high school you happily finds the keys in your jeans pocket by the laundry hamper. Late for an end of the year kegger with your boyfriend in college, you frantically trip over empty pizza boxes and video game controllers before finding them wedged tightly between couch cushions.

But as you race around it slowly and painfully dawns on you one by one by one . . .

Those places are all empty today.

Spotlights meet and then dim on your sad and hollow face as the audience suddenly realizes it's a tragedy. The curtain drops heavily and there is quiet and respectable applause from those who aren't too shocked to show their appreciation.

But wait . . .

The theater lights stay down, there is some quick whispering, a tiny sizzle of electricity fills the room.

There is an encore!

The curtain lifts for a final fleeting scene of you scrambling around your house trying to form some **drippy, half-baked plan.** You consider calling in sick for the day, getting your girlfriend to come home so you can copy her keys, or changing the locks altogether.

As you race around with your jacket, a tipped-over laundry basket and strewn couch cushions all over the floor, the music gets faster as you scale higher and higher toward **complete lunacy.**

Nearly in tears and on the verge of madness, sweat drips down your face as you suddenly swing open the door with full force and then gasp as you immediately spot them: **hanging in the lock.**

The audience leaps to their feet and erupts, filling the theater with **booming applause,** loud whistles, and screams from the balcony.

You smile at them and wink, grab the keys, **kiss them,** and hold them to the sky. Then you run onto the driveway, jump in your car, and zoom off into the distance.

Trumpets blast from the pit band, the standing ovation continues, and big bouquets of bright red roses are tossed onstage as the great play ends with a flourish.

And sure, when this happens in real life you feel stupid, ashamed, and guilty, but **more than anything else** you feel a sweet sense of relief. Your muscles droop, your chest unclenches, and a tidal wave rushes inside you and fills you up with joy.

When you finally find your keys after looking forever, you hear the audience hooting and hollering as the curtain closes on this perfect little scene of

AWESOME!

Eating the extra fries at the bottom of the bag

Hey, eating in the car is tough.

Weaving that **bulky clunk of metal** through highway traffic, off off-ramps, and into parallel parking spots is no small feat. And you know what makes it worse? Having a **hot, crumpled bag** of steamy drive-thru riding shotgun, that's what.

Yes, resisting the temptation is tough, but then again unwrapping a **sloppy mustard-dripping burger** over the steering wheel probably isn't good for anybody. So there's really only one option to satisfy your urges to both **eat and live**.

That's right: Dip your hand in the crinkly paper well and squeeze between cool packets of ketchup, big wads of napkins, and waxy-wrapped burgers until you find that treasure trove of fries at the bottom of the bag. It's like panning for gold and is known as the **Pre-Lunch Munch** in some circles.

Also, we can't forget the **Classic Afterburn** move. Yes, bag fries star again, but this time they're the limp 'n' salty chasers after your last slurp of bland watered-down cola. Yes, we both know you've got to finish that off with a **flavor-saving punch**, and bonus fries will do the job just fine.

So dig that hand in deep and pull out a nice little bite of AWESOME!

The feeling of scrunching sand in your feet

....

Free your feet.

When you kick off your tight, suffocating shoes, peel off your **sweaty socks**, and just starting walking on the beach in bare feet, how good does that feel?

Man, it's a million molecules of Earthbeads massaging your foot all at once. It's a tickly, grippy sand sensation. It's big piles of small cubes hugging and comforting your tired and **broken soles.**

And yeah, sure, the sand wedges itself up into your toenails and coats the bottom of your feet like butter on toast. But whatever, because the feeling of scrunching sand in your feet when you walk on the beach is certifiably

AWESOME!

Scraping all the lint off an overflowing lint trap

....

There's something therapeutic about finger-peeling that **dark-gray-with-red-flecks** fuzz patch off the trap, rolling it into a ball, and tossing it in the trash. Yes, after you ditch that **hot, furry blanket**, both you and your dryer can finally breathe again.

AWESOME!

The thank-you wave when you let somebody merge in front of you

....

Cruising with our music cranked and our cell phones ringing, we sometimes find it hard to communicate with other drivers sharing the roads. When speeds are high and time's a'ticking, we rely on silent gestures to get our points across.

Now, we all know the Thank-You Wave when you let someone merge in front of you is a great move. It's **highway payment** for arriving at your destination **one car length later** whenever you let someone in.

But it doesn't end there.

Sure, courtesy-wave etiquette may have started with the post-merge Thank-You Wave, but the magic has spread:

1. **The Red Light Squeeze Wave.** You pull up to a red light and the guy in front of you squeezes into the intersection a bit so you can make your right turn faster. As you pull up and make your move, it's time to thank that special someone for shaving twenty seconds off your commute.

2. **The Pre-Wave.** As in I'm thanking you because the

front tip of my Honda Civic is pointed into your traffic-jammed lane and I know you see me so just let me in. Sure, you can try to avoid eye contact, but I'm determined to Pre-Wave you to build up some goodwill.

3. **The Apology Wave.** Don't be fooled: Even though it looks similar to the thank-you wave, the apology wave is typically accompanied by a big grimace instead of an eyebrow raise. Next time you side-swipe a van of teenagers and send them skidding off the highway into a roadside ditch, be sure to offer a **heartfelt** apology wave.

4. **The Go-Ahead Wave.** You roll up to a four-way stop at the same time as another car and decide to let them turn first. Maybe they're a sweet old lady barely peeking over the wheel or maybe you just want to avoid The World's Slowest Car Accident. Either way, you give them the pleasant, open-palmed Go-Ahead Wave, which is sort of how the ladies on *The Price Is Right* unveil a new washer and dryer set.

Proper courtesy-wave etiquette keeps two-way talking alive on our streets and prevents chaos from ruling the laneways. So when you do something generous keep watch for a wave, and when someone helps you out be sure to smile and wave right back.

AWESOME!

When you're really tired and about to fall asleep and someone throws a blanket on you

....

Hey, you know what's even better than taking a nap on the couch? Well, I'll tell you: that feeling you get **just before** you fall asleep on the couch.

Yes, that's when you enter that blissful, semiconscious **Pre-Nap World** where your thoughts float and zoom around your brain and your muscles relax and detensify. The sun feels warm on your face, the radio in the background fades to a comforting white noise, and you know . . . you just know . . . that you're about to fall asleep.

It feels great.

There are really only two things that can disturb you when you're in the Pre-Nap World:

1. **Feeling like you have to go to the bathroom.** Sorry, but unless you trust your bladder to balloon without bursting, you might just have to get up for this one. Nobody can really help you go to the bathroom while you're lying on the couch, unless they really, really love you.

2. **Feeling cold.** You get those ol' lying-on-the-couch shivers. You know your sheets and blankets are back on your bed, and you could just get up to get them, but you don't really want to move because then you'll leave the blissful Pre-Nap World. And it's a nice world. It's a world you don't leave lightly.

So that's why it's great whenever someone notices your dilemma and just quietly grabs a blanket from the closet and tosses it on your semiconscious self. If they're really nice, they even **flap the blanket above you** and let it open up and softly land on you.

When that happens, you immediately feel the warmth radiating around you, a tiny smile curls itself on the corners of your lips, and you fall deeper and deeper into a nice, relaxing rest.

AWESOME!

Getting your ID checked when you're way over the legal age

···

Hey, sometimes you're in the mood for a few drinks.

Big bottle of merlot over a romantic spaghetti dinner, clinking beers floating in an icy cooler beside the tent, **Jell-O shooters** before the bars in college, or bubbly flutes of champagne for the big New Year's bash.

Whatever your pleasure, whatever your poison, that's cool with us. But before you get down with the booze-filled pour, you need to get out that door and run down to the liquor store. Word to your sister.

Now, if you're like me, you go through four distinct phases when you get your ID checked, and they go a little something like this:

- **Stage 1: Underage Rage.** Okay, you're not quite at the legal limit but you're close enough to push it. Problem is that the pimply dude at the cash register ain't buying your fake ID and you get busted at the scene. So close yet so far. You storm away with your Friday night plans dashed, burning with a bit of underage rage.

- **Stage 2: New Booze Buzz.** When you hit the legal limit, it's time to fight for your right to party. You wheel your shopping cart around the store with pride, picking up a bit of this, a bit of that, and beaming like a schoolgirl when the cashier asks for your ID. "Why, no problem at all!" you say loudly, grinning widely at the tired, bleary-eyed folks behind you in line. "Thank you so much for asking!"

- **Stage 3: Jaded Twentysomething.** You're four or five years over the limit and the novelty has worn off. Now it's becoming a pain to dig through your wallet to find your driver's license before scooting home with a six-pack for the game. Can't the clerk clearly see you're twenty-six? Does he think you could have grown that goatee five years ago?

- **Stage 4: The Fountain of Youth.** After a while, the gray hairs add up and you start buying white wine for the backyard barbecue instead of lollipop-flavored vodka coolers for the all-night rager. You know your way around the store, you smile warmly at the clerk, and suddenly you get asked for your ID when you least expect it.

Oh baby, when it hasn't happened in years, getting your ID checked can be a **full body buzz**. You fish out your card excitedly, peeling its faded face and dog-eared corners from your bag, and your eyes twinkle as you take a sip from the fountain of youth.

Sometimes it even happens on your birthday.

AWESOME!

The smell of rain on a hot sidewalk

There's just something about the smell of rain on a hot sidewalk. It's sort of like the rain cleans the air—completely hammering all the dirt and grime particles down to the ground and releasing some hot **baked-in chemicals** from the pavement. It smells best if it hasn't rained in a while and the sidewalk is scalding hot. Then it sort of **sizzles and steams** up into a big, hot, intoxicating whiff.

AWESOME!

That friendly nod between strangers out doing the same thing

....

Gliding down the bike path on a Saturday morning, you whip by somebody peddling in the opposite direction and give each other a nod. For a moment it's like "Hey, we're both doing the same thing. Let's be friends for a second."

Also applies to seeing someone driving the same car as you, walking their dog past you on Sunday morning, or squeezing the melon beside you in the grocery store.

AWESOME!

Really, really old Tupperware

Found in dusty kitchen cupboards and dishwasher top shelves across this wide, great land, really, really old Tupperware is as handy today as it was twenty, thirty, forty years ago. That famous Tupperware **burping seal** still holds strong, and you can bet that banana bread will stay moist, those celery sticks crisp, and that leftover lasagna fresh. Yes, all is well in this tight vacuum-sealed **Chamber of Taste Preservation**.

Really, really old Tupperware is mostly found in three colors: Stovetop Green, **Traffic Cone Orange**, or The Core Of The Sun Yellow. Optional features include novelty 1950s floral patterns or deep tomato stains from that time someone put chili in there and shoved it in the back of the freezer for two years.

One thing I enjoy doing is thinking about all the different kinds of food a particular piece of Tupperware has Tupperwared shut over the years. Apparently Tupperware has been around since 1946, so we're talking about the full tastebud time line—from lard burgers, creamed-corn casseroles, and **Jell-O salads** to hemp brownies, parsley soup, and tofu cookies to pizza pockets, TV dinner leftovers, and astronaut ice cream pellets.

Really, really old Tupperware has been there, sealed that,

and lived to tell the tale. It's a throwback to the simpler life, when things like airtight seals meant something. Something real. Something honest.

Something worth believing in.

AWESOME!

Getting gas just before the price goes up

....

Here's how it all goes down.

Well-dressed fat cats sit around a dark, mahogany table in the boardroom of a **nondescript high-rise** deep in a dense metropolis on the coast of an exotic country. Anonymous and alone, they sip scotch, share pictures of new yachts, and **make plans to jack gas prices** for the long weekend.

Cuff links clinking on crystal glasses, **celebratory cigar smoke** filling the room, the gas execs laugh deep belly laughs, high ten each other, and then file into limos to take them back to the airport. And of course, just before they leave, everyone does a shot of **high-octane gasoline** to keep the memory fresh and the evil juices flowing.

At least that's how I imagine it.

After all, gas prices seemingly rise whenever you need to fill up for the weekend. It's a constant game and a constant battle.

But that's why there's something fun about watching those prices drip and drop ever so slowly throughout the week and then **pulling in to fill your tank just before they zoom sky-high again.**

Honestly, when you nail it just right you walk away laughing, patting the extra three dollars in your pocket and daydreaming of how you might spend it this time. Lottery ticket, **windshield washer fluid**, maybe some beef jerky for the ride home. Either way, you'll be sitting pretty when you cruise by the station on a full tank tomorrow and notice the prices are hiked back up.

You came out to play the **Gas Game** this week.

And you won.

AWESOME!

The pushoff

Dad's holding you steady as you pedal, pedal, pedal. Then you suddenly realize you're still going, so you look over your shoulder and he's way back there, waving and cheering you on.

You're riding your bike for the first time.

AWESOME!

Wearing sandals when you shouldn't be wearing sandals

I went to college in a small town that got hit hard by weather extremes.

In the **fall**, the summer winds would quickly cool and sharpen, ripping into your cheeks on the way home from class, leaving them red and finely shredded like you'd just applied blush with sandpaper.

In the **winter**, the roads and sidewalks would be covered in piles of wet slush—little bombs of slippery ice-dirt and road salt that would explode onto your pants and shoes and leave nasty stains when they dried.

In the **spring,** the snow would melt away, leaving soggy grass everywhere. You would see that grass and think it was solid, but your foot would sink into it, cold little mud bubbles rising around your shoe from all directions and soaking right into your sock. It was like walking on a peat bog covered in smushed worms and last year's dog poo.

It was not pretty. And so my roommates and I were left with just two options:

1. Try to predict and adjust for the weather. You know, wear lots of layers, carry umbrellas on sunny days,

build a collection of waterproof boots, and start using phrases like "bunker in" and "venture out."

2. Ignore it completely.

Well, we chose Option 2.

And we faced the consequences.

We got windburn and had sleet slip down the back of our T-shirts. We got **dirt soakers** and permanently stretched our socks while peeling them off at the front door. We got dry legs, we got bone chill, and, brother, we got **rain hair** bad.

But eventually we got good at ignoring it all.

My roommate Dee was the master of ignoring the weather, the biggest proof being that **he wore sandals year-round**. Wind, snow, rain, it didn't matter. "The toes need to breathe," he'd say sternly, "breathe." And he'd emphasize the point with a sturdy lip and a firm strapping of the Velcro. Then he'd slap on his heavy backpack, take a deep breath, give you a wink, and trudge out into a blizzard, navigating ice patches and slush piles like a pro.

Sure, there was the occasional **Bad Day** that came with being chronically unprepared for Mother Nature's worst blows, generally involving a **dirty-puddle splashing** all over you from a passing truck or being unable to feel your toes until you put them on the radiator for twenty minutes. But you made it through.

And come on, there is something really great about wearing sandals when you shouldn't be wearing sandals. It's liberation from shoe shackles, **freedom from the oppressing sock**, and a violent rebellion against those frostbite warnings on the weather channel.

People of the world, let's face it: If we can come together to take down the shoe, then really, nothing can stop us.

AWESOME!

Getting off an airplane after a long flight

....

B.O. clouds dissipate and float away, **wailing babies quit wailing at the luggage bay**, your cell phone works, so you call friends up, say hey, and all your scrunched-up, **bunched-up**, hunched-up muscles just relax as you stretch them out now, feeling **A-OK**. You're out of the window seat, out of the aisle, you're back on two feet, so just walk away and smile.

AWESOME!

Picking up a *q* and *u* at the same time in Scrabble

I'm the world's worst Scrabble player.

Every time it's my turn I see other players lose interest as they get ready for a long wait. I feel bad, so I stare at my pieces, trying desperately to conjure up a word longer than three letters or else suffer their complaints that I'm "really clogging up the board." A couple minutes will pass before somebody says, "Hey, you know what this game should have? **A time limit**, ha ha ha ha ha!!!" And everybody laughs and smiles at me, and I look up to grin and then stare back down at my letters quickly. I stare at those letters and stare hard. A few more minutes of silence will pass, and then I look up, grimace slowly, and offer one of my two classic lines:

1. "Sorry guys, I've got like all vowels over here," or
2. "It's like Consonant Central here, guys. I'll be just another minute unless jgrfqll is a word."

A couple people nod and smile at my lame joke, someone idly turns on the TV and starts flipping channels, and another will generally grab a section of the newspaper and head to the can. I frantically rearrange my letters over and over again, silently praying *rebuke, jinxed,* or *fibula* will appear on my little wooden tray by accident.

My nerves fraying, my heart drum-thumping, I'll eventually put down a lame four-letter word like *bill* or *lamp* in an act of desperation. "Eight points," I'll whisper to the scorekeeper, while turning the board and nodding to the other players to move along.

See, part of my problem is that I draw letters like *j, z,* or *q* at the beginning of the game and they end up haunting me all the way through. **That big *q* is the worst of all.** It holds its powerful 10 points over my head, just daring me to draw one of the four *u*'s in the game so I can lay it down. I spell my letters out in arrangements like *q_ick, q_ote,* and *q_iet,* ready and waiting for a *u* at any time, but generally no dice, or at least no dice for a while. I got *qat* or I got nothing.

And so you see that's why, in my books, there are very few better **Things to Happen to You in a Board Game** than picking a *q* and a *u* at the same time in Scrabble. I say it beats building two hotels on Boardwalk in Monopoly or drawing a perfect brontosaurus in Pictionary during an All Play.

If I get that *q* and *u* together in Scrabble, then it's all me all the time, baby. Doors open, and I quite quietly and quickly quash all quibbling questions and quack queries from my competitors.

And you know how that makes me feel.

AWESOME!

Old folks who sit on their porch and wave at you when you walk by

What do you picture doing when you retire?

Lounging amongst big umbrellas on **sunny beaches**, taking the grandkids to the zoo, cropping a serious **vegetable garden**, or turning your woodcarving hobby into a lucrative craft fair business?

Well, whatever you choose, can I recommend that you also make time to just sit on your porch, **sip some lemonade**, and look up to smile and wave at people when they walk by?

Because other than cutting the little wedge of your neighbor's lawn, lending out your snowblower, or collecting someone's mail while they're away, I tell you: Nothing says friendly neighbor more than a couple old folks sitting on their rockers and just flashing those gums and waving those palms when you walk on by.

AWESOME!

The first scoop out of a jar of peanut butter

....

When I peel the top off a new jar of peanut butter I like to pretend **I'm a scientist** peering through the world's most powerful telescope, catching Earth's first glimpse of a new, strange and distant planet. "It's got a smooth surface," I exclaim to the lab of giddy professors standing breathlessly beside me. "Yes, it's a **beautiful airless landscape**, untouched, undisturbed, and brown."

Because seriously, that's what a just-opened jar of peanut butter looks like to me. I almost feel bad thinking about what I'm about to do, because it's just so perfect, smooth, and dense. But I put some bread in the toaster anyway, grab a spoon from the drawer, and then go right ahead and dig that spoon in there deep, catching a heavy glob of thick PB when I pull up, **a loud, wet, satisfying** schthlop plopping out of the jar.

It's a great feeling.

After that, I'm an artist. I can leave a **big, gaping hole** right in the middle of the jar, I can do it up fancy and **twirl and swirl** the PB around a little, or I can painstakingly **carve a moat** around the outside, leaving a perfect, flat island in the center that becomes more and more unstable with every passing day.

The options are unlimited.

Really, I think getting the first dig in a jar of peanut butter is the kitchen equivalent of **stabbing a flag into the moon** and claiming it as your own. I mean, you mark that peanut butter. **You brand it.** You add your little stamp and you put it back in the pantry, ready and waiting for the next big schthlop.

AWESOME!

Hearing a stranger fart in public

What's funnier than hearing a stranger fart in public?

Well sure, it can happen in a bank lineup, hotel lobby, or subway car. It can happen in a restaurant, movie theater, or local bar. But the funniest of all has got to be the **Elevator Fart**. That's the king of public farts, for two main reasons:

1. **Acoustics.** It's almost always dead silent in an elevator. People usually keep quiet, stare firmly at the front door, and wait for their floor. Any whisper or laugh echoes around the box with full force, reverberating loudly for all to hear. So a giant rippling fart popped out by a bald businessman in a suit holding a briefcase in front of him? That's like a 21-gun salute.

2. **Time.** If you're climbing a high-rise, you're spending maybe a minute or two with these people. It's you and them, locked together. Hearing a stranger fart on the sidewalk is one thing. Hearing a stranger fart in a tiny enclosed room is another. Nobody can escape the full experience, from big bang to first whiff to total elevator saturation.

Hearing a stranger fart in public is great partly because of everybody's reaction. **There are really four main types of fart reactions you see:**

- **Concealed Laughers.** These folks purse their lips tightly, pop open their eyes, and try not to laugh. If they're with friends, then the sight of their friend also trying to hold in a laugh can be too much, and they suddenly explode into full-blown belly laughs.

- **The Business Class.** Folks in suits often try to pretend that nothing happened. "Nope, everything's just chipper here, I don't smell anything at all." Their only tells might be a very subtle step away from the culprit and a few extra looks at their watches.

- **Deep-Sea Divers.** These folks try to hold their breath as long as possible. They hear the fart and it's "Come on, lungs, don't fail me now." They're the ones with the chipmunk cheeks who eventually pop and gasp desperately for air when the door opens.

- **Innocent Children.** Little kids are always the funniest. I once heard a child in an elevator say, "Mommy, that man just farted," with a full-on finger point right into the well-dressed ass in front of his face. But hey, I guess if you're going to fart in a kid's face, you deserve to be called out.

Yes, hearing a stranger fart in public can be a **tiny, hilarious moment** in the middle of any day. If you're the farter, I say be loud and be proud! We've all been there, so no need to be embarrassed. If you're in the audience, I say enjoy the **hilarious social faux pas** and resulting reaction in the room.

So thank you, strangers farting in public, for adding a great bit of comic relief to the middle of our day.

AWESOME!

Perfectly toasted toast

A bad burn and you've got black crumbs and a dry middle. A lukewarm bake and you've got a **gummy center** and soft crusts. So push the button down, twiddle the knob, and dial up some perfection.

AWESOME!

When someone unjams the photocopier for you

A jammed photocopier at the office is a terrible scene.

Toner fumes fill the air, plastic doors are swung open, and crumpled papers lie wedged tightly in the machine's **Plinko board torso** of hot springs and **bright green clasps**.

And there you stand at the **scene of the crime** in your pleated pants and button-down shirt. Yeah, I'm guessing the last thing you feel like doing right now is dropping to your **hands and knees** and poking your fingers into that steaming engine of paper trays and twirly knobs.

That's what makes it so great when a bugle blares softly in the background and out pops the **King of the Office** from around the cubicle wall. Yes, it's **Unjammer Man**, that young techie kid from the IT department who declogs the photocopier in no time flat and is happy to lend a hand.

Your lips curl into a big smile and you hug your expense report, while knobs are twiddled, **clasps are fiddled**, and the copier quickly starts humming like brand new.

Now that someone's unjammed it for you, you're back in business, baby.

And you're loving it.

AWESOME!

Reading the nutritional label and eating it anyway

....

Sometimes you just gotta peek.

As you unwrap the chocolate bar, peel open the cheeseburger, or scoop up that second bowl of ice cream, you can't help but turn the package around to glance at the **nutritional label** on the back.

And guess what's waiting for you over there? You got it, baby: 64 percent of your daily **saturated fat** intake, 76 percent of your cholesterol, and a couple big buckets of carbs.

Then there's the quick pause, involuntary **eye twitch**, or ashamed look at the person munching salad beside you. But I hope after that brief moment of self-doubt, you just keep going, you just keep scooping it in. Sure, you might have to turn the label away, avoid sodium for the rest of the day, or give a shrug and say, "Hey, it's okay," but I hope you keep going, hope you savor it slowly, and hope you enjoy every last bite.

Sometimes you just gotta read the nutritional label and eat it anyway.

Sometimes . . . you just gotta live.

AWESOME!

When you're watching one of your favorite movies and you realize you don't remember how it ends

You know the feeling.

Your favorite characters are introduced, the story kicks off, a couple plot twists and turns seem a bit unfamiliar, and it suddenly dawns on you: You have **no clue** how the movie wraps up. No, you can't remember who the killer is, who dies, or if the cats ever get married. You can't remember the ending at all, and you're loving every minute of it.

So you dim the lights, **snuggle under the blanket**, shush up your chatty husband, and stay glued to that screen.

Because it's like, hey, **guaranteed blockbuster**.

AWESOME!

The smell of the coffee aisle in the grocery store

Harsh fluorescent lighting, slushy wet floors, and the cloudy **stench of raw fish** welcome you into your friendly neighborhood grocery store. After circling tables of **green bananas**, wobbly paper towel towers, and piles of day-old bagels, it's kind of nice to stumble upon the coffee aisle and just take a big sniff.

AWESOME!

That pile of assorted beers left in your fridge after a party

My friend Mike has rules for hosting parties. They go like this:

- **Under 25 years old:** Party is BYOB. You can tell people if you want, but they should know. Bring your own beer. Bring your own mix. Bring your own bulk-pack cheesy puffs.
- **25-30 years old:** Host should have wine and beer stocked and there should be snacks available. You're an old fart now, so there's a bit more party responsibility. Try to squeeze a trip in to pick up some booze between renewing your mortgage and seeing the doctor about your kidney stones.
- **30-40 years old:** All of the above plus an open bar. If you follow Mike's rules, this decade is going to hit the pocketbook a little bit.
- **Over 40 years old:** Open bar plus catering staff. Prime time, baby.

But those are his rules.

My rules are: If you're coming over, bring a chair. See,

because we rarely provide people with anything. No drinks, no seating, no toilet paper in the bathroom, and definitely no old butler with a pencil mustache walking around in tails asking if you'd like an endive covered in swan liver and truffle oil.

Instead we stick a piece of paper on the front door telling you to meet us in the back, and then help you get started on the two six-packs you brought over. If you're lucky, we might have a leftover bag of stale nachos kicking around or maybe some puddings in the cupboard. If not, we'll need **your credit card** to order a pizza.

I am an extremely cheap person, so I get a kick out of the random assortment of drinks left over in the fridge the morning after a party. You can basically play detective to figure out who came the night before: buzzy energy drink with vodka (night-shift worker trying to stay up), cans of domestic beer (grad student on a budget), oversized brown bottles with flip-top stoppers and lots of consonants on the label (yuppie couple or Europeans), sugary vodka coolers (college girls), craft beers with names like Old Flag or Rocky Tundra (hipsters), fancy bottles of port (British Conservative Party).

Man, I love that random mishmash of assorted beers and drinks in the fridge. Mostly because it makes me feel like a better host next time people come over.

AWESOME!

Staring out at calm water

AWESOME!

Blowing out all the candles on your first try

Keep the spit to yourself and just let it fly. It's time to get windy.

AWESOME!

Sneaking McDonald's and hiding the evidence

....

Trouble bubbled at my friend Scott's house one night.

See, earlier in the week Scott found a used **McDonald's Chicken McNugget** sauce container wedged between the car seat and the door in the Honda Civic he shares with his wife. He dropped his keys in there, and when he slipped his hand down to fish them out, he came up with a sticky, crusty **barbecue sauce** container instead.

His wife Molly was caught grease-handed. In Scott's mind their sturdy **New Year's pact** to eat healthy suddenly dissolved into a dimly lit puddle of lies and deception.

Lucky for me, Scott decided to raise the issue one Monday night while we were all watching TV.

Here's how it went down.

> **Scott:** "Oh hey, I dropped my keys in that annoying spot between the car seat and the car door earlier today."
>
> **Molly:** *(curious as to where this is going)* "Okay . . ."
>
> **Scott:** "Yeah, but when I went to pull them out, I found something else instead."
>
> **Molly:** *(slightly confused)* "O-kay . . . ?"

Scott: *(raises eyebrows slowly and smiles)*

Molly: *(scrunches eyebrow and turns head in confusion)*

Scott: "A McDonald's barbecue sauce container!"

Molly: *(guiltily)* "Oh! Nooo . . ."

Then there was a short, silent pause.

And then we all just burst out laughing.

Because, seriously, we've all been there, man. Sneaking in those secret **McDonald's Drive-Thru** trips and ditching the evidence. Yup, gotta make sure you've scooped all the fries off the bottom of the bag, **wiped the salt** off your lips, checked your shirt for **ketchup spillage**, and safely filed the excess napkins away in the glove compartment. It's a delicious guilty pleasure and your secret is safe with us.

Just remember to roll down the windows, **pay with cash**, and play it safe out there.

And never ever order the nuggets.

AWESOME!

Your family car growing up

Hanging out with friends late, late, late one night, dim music playing in the background, **splayed haphazardly** on a fat, squishy couch, my brother-in-law Dee started waxing nostalgic about his family's big, old **1991 white Chevy Suburban**.

He just broke into it too.

"That monster seated nine people, I swear to you. Honestly, nine! There was a bench in the back, a bench in the middle, and **a bench in the front**. I remember when my parents bought it, I said, 'Why not get the captain's chairs in the front?' and they were like, 'No, that's just not practical.' But I guess the benches did come in handy. My dad drove our entire baseball team around. Fourteen **twelve-year-olds** wedged in tight and twisted. We called it The Team Tank. Ha ha, honestly man, I miss that old beast."

And then he just smiled softly, shook his head, and stared absently at the remote control on the coffee table for a minute.

Dee's wistful late-night rambles got me thinking.

For my sister Nina and me, nothing beat sitting in the backseat of our **1984 Pontiac Station Wagon** with brown paint, brown interior, and classy **fake wood trim** on the outside. The backseat in this Logmobile was about eight feet away from the driver but a world apart, really. You could talk and play games out of earshot, all the while looking and laughing straight out the back window, distracting people behind you on the highway.

In the summer the **metal belt buckles** would grow red-hot and scald your skin when you buckled up. The cup holders were full of sticky remains from the half-dozen spilled Cokes that didn't get sponged up by the handful of McDonald's napkins stuffed in there. The air conditioning was temperamental, the windows wouldn't roll down all the way, and there were no entertainment systems or talking maps. You invented your own fun and sat patiently on the dark fabric seats, deeply stained from the time somebody **sat on a hot banana**.

So what was your car? Was it a **'69 Dodge Dart**? A Chevette in Classic Dull Gray or '95 Chevy Lumina van? Was it a monstrous '68 Impala, a '54 DeSoto, or a bright teal '91 **Ford Taurus**?

Whatever it was, I bet it sure does give you a trip down memory lane when you see that car, **the same color**, the same style, just driving around town like nobody's business. Or maybe fixed up real nice at the antique car show.

Or maybe coasting calmly on cruise through your brain every so often.

Steering up some memories.

AWESOME!

Eating a free sample of something you have no intention of buying

....

Why hello, little cup of strawberry-kiwi punch. How **you** doing, pepper-dill crackers? Don't mind if I do, tiny salami wrapped around a piece of melon.

Yes, eating a free sample of something you have no intention of buying is a great way to stay on top of what's happening in the grocery store. You swish the new drink, chew the new gum, toss back a tiny cup of the new **pasta dinner**, and introduce your tastebuds to a little surprise.

Assuming you don't actually like the product, maybe you do what I do and pretend you're going to buy it anyway so you don't hurt the sweet, heavily lipsticked **Sample Lady's** feelings. So you pick up the box of dry crackers, salty salami, or all-noodle-no-cheese lasagna and say, "Hmmm. $4.29? Not bad, not bad. And I get a fifty-cents-off coupon too? Hmmm." Then you smile back at her, toss it in your cart, and say, "Why not! Thank you very much!"

Then you roll out of sight and guiltily drop it in another aisle.

AWESOME!

Sneaking under someone else's umbrella

Okay, who's the smart one who brought an umbrella? Because I know it's not me.

No, when the sky cracks up and the rain smacks down, I'm the one wearing heavy jeans and a **thick, spongy sweater** that soaks up everything and turns me into a **swampy slab of peat bog**. I'm drenched, I'm dripping, I'm ice-chilled to the bone.

But that's what makes it so great when it starts coming down and out pops a giant umbrella from a friend who offers to gimme shelter for a few minutes. Yes, if your special someone is packing some **giant nylon heat**, then I think it's fair to say you're smiling high, your clothes are dry, and you're rocking the streets under a tiny little patch of

AWESOME!

Finally remembering a word that's been on the tip of your tongue for so long

....

It's like throwing a pail of cold water on all your smoking inner head parts. Gears unjam, lines start rolling, and you settle back in the restaurant booth with a satisfied smile on your face and just blurt it out.

"Parcheesi, that's what it was called."

AWESOME!

When someone offers to toss your dirty clothes in with their load of laundry

....

While flipping channels mindlessly one day, I ended up at the Fast Money round of *Family Feud* just as the host said to the contestant, "Name a household chore you don't mind doing."

The contestant flashed a split-second look of **massive confusion** before reluctantly spitting out an answer. When it was the second guy's turn to answer it, he flashed the same look. One ended up saying **vacuuming** and the other went with **washing the dishes**. Neither got the top answer, which was **doing laundry**, so they unfortunately went home with empty pockets flipped inside out with flies buzzing out of them.

But you know what? I'm with them. Who knew people liked laundry? That can't be true. For me, laundry has two major strikes against it:

1. **Time.** Laundry requires a huge time investment. You can't just set it and forget it like our trusty old pal Dishwasher. No, washing clothes means an afternoon in and out of the laundry room or a night reading tabloids at the laundromat. And you have

to be on the ball, ready to rebalance the washer, move clothes to the dryer, and fold shirts before they get wrinkled.

2. **Effort.** I am baffled by the laundry sorting process and have trouble interpreting that fancy hiero-glyphic **Triangle Square Circle** language somebody invented to ruin my clothes.

For all these reasons it's great when you're lazily watching *Family Feud* on the couch and your spouse, roommate, or sibling trucks by carrying a basket full of clothes. If you're lucky enough to get that **"Hey, need to throw anything in here?"** then it's show time so get going!

You have maybe a minute or two before the washer starts filling up, so now's your chance to drop everything, run to your dirty clothes, and start flinging out the bare minimum you need to get by for a few days. Do it fast, run back to the laundry room, and thank them profusely as you toss your clothes in the pile.

Then it's back to the couch for the Triple Money round, where you can rest easy knowing you'll have some freshly rinsed undies for tomorrow morning.

AWESOME!

The moment at a restaurant after you see your food coming from the kitchen but before it lands on your table

....

Somebody shushes, **conversation hushes**, and all eyes flicker with delight as you watch your sizzling, glistening meals cruise out of the kitchen and slowly descend in front of you.

AWESOME!

Terrible businesses
run by children

When I was about fourteen years old, I signed up for something called **Junior Achievement**. It was a happy-go-lucky nonprofit group that promoted business and entrepreneurship skills in children. Or basically, it was a bunch of kids in a room every Thursday night acting like **middle managers** with adult supervision.

My group came up with a business called Roc Creations. This was a clever play on our core product: cheap, homemade rock necklaces. We thought it was a brilliant, failsafe plan. After all, who likes necklaces? Everybody, of course. And how cheap are rocks? Pretty darn cheap, man. We spent one Thursday **at the beach**, the next one painting, and a final Thursday drilling holes and tying string through them. We figured it was a solid plan, well executed.

Sadly, after a few weeks we realized we'd made a huge mistake. We bet all our chips on a losing hand. The necklaces failed to generate enough buzz and excitement at the flea markets, despite our screaming rhyming chants at **terrified housewives**, and we quickly tumbled into the red, large piles of dead inventory and **drill bit invoices** mocking our poor judgment.

But then, like any good business, we evolved. We quickly changed our name to **Roc-Cal Creations** and printed off a quickie run of **cheapo laminated calendars**. We tied on a dry-erase marker, slapped some magnets on the back, and went door-to-door, neighbor-to-neighbor, selling these **reusable fridge calendars** for four bucks a pop.

Well, we managed to sell enough to get back in gear. We started to make money and established a strong partnership with the lady in the **markers aisle at Staples**. Yes, it all ended well, but not without some late nights under a dim lamp with a dollar-store calculator, a stack of graph paper, and a pile of **pencil crayons**, trying desperately to finish the numbers for our annual report, which was actually printed on the inside of one of our folded-up calendars.

It was a great experience and it really got **my buzz going** for running a business. That's why I think it's always fun when you see children running some sort of strange, hilarious, or terrible business. Because really, you're just watching them learn things they don't learn in the classroom and have fun doing it. They're learning how to sell, picking up social skills, and jumping right into the whirring gears of the marketplace. And honestly, they're doing all this by just getting out there and giving it a shot.

How cute are the twins **selling lemonade** on the street corner? The gymnastics team running the barbecue outside the mall? Or the kid who takes your grocery cart back if he gets to keep the twenty-five-cent deposit?

Those kids are all playing the game. So we say: Go on, kids. Do it well. Next time you're selling some rock-hard cookies or salty date squares at a bake sale, sign us up. Because we're not just buying some mild indigestion, are we?

No, we're investing in the future.

AWESOME!

Frozen walls of air conditioning hitting you on hot days

Sometimes after a day of walking around in **blistering summer heat,** I come down with a bad case of **Gross Face**.

People, I'm not proud of it, but on those steamy days a nasty combination of shiny forehead sweat, downtown street air, and dried-up sunblock gives me a mask I can't shake. Yes, my otherwise flawless, milky-smooth complexion gets slathered with **the drips**, and suddenly I'm cruising around town with pit stains and a T-shirt sweat-glued to my back.

If you been there, you know it's a sticky, sweaty slog.

But there is good news.

Invisible, frozen walls of cranked air conditioning exist just beyond the front door of the nearest coffee shop, post office, or **convenience store**. Just pop in to experience a frigid slap of ice-cold air right in the kisser.

When you find these hidden gems of subzero bliss, it's like momentarily trading your **slimy sweat mask** for a new face. Glistening, wet necks get an **ice-cold sponge down**, stinging eyelids freeze to ice, and your disgusting hot-baked face gives a relaxing smile as it's shotgun-blasted with a chilly round of

AWESOME!

Catching somebody singing in their car and sharing a laugh with them

It's late, it's quiet, and you're stuck at a red light.

Casually, you glance to your left and notice a muted explosion of furious head bopping, furrowed eyebrows, and silent wailing inside, as the driver rocks out alone and in the zone.

And there's just something worth smiling about when you observe that passionate display of **pure private pleasure** only a few feet away. Suddenly you're the producer in the booth watching your struggling artist hit the high notes in their tight **sound chamber on wheels**. Yes, they've tried for years to get clean and make it off the streets, but now you're finally smelling a hit . . .

. . . and a future.

So maybe you bop along for a few beats, catch the same song on your radio, or lock eyes with them for a second and share a warm and heartfelt laugh. Maybe you feel **a tiny flip** in your heart as you connect with a total stranger for a few fleeting seconds. And maybe it makes you a tiny bit happier and maybe you smile a tiny bit more.

I say we salute all the **highway rockers** of the world. Thanks for brightening our day and making us laugh at the reds. Rock on and keep belting them out, because you make the world shine brighter and make our long drives home a lot more

AWESOME!

Snow stepping

Snow stepping is when you're trudging through the snow wearing shoes, but someone ahead of you wore boots so you get to step in all the nice **Snow Holes** they made for you.

AWESOME!

Taking off your shoes on a long car ride

....

Treat your feet.

Say you're enjoying the backseat of the car, your **shaggy locks** whipping in the wind, your hand sailing carelessly out the window, and your head lightly bopping to the faint **Buddy Holly** tune on the AM dial.

But your feet, they are not fine, they are not carefree, and they ain't bopping to no beat. No, they're slippery, salty, and sweaty, wrapped tightly in a **hot pocket** of suffocating socks and shoes. Yes, buried deep under dense layers of cotton, wool, and leather, your aching soles are itching for some sweet release and a breath of fresh air.

So just let them out, friend.

Yes, when the car slips onto the side roads, the bus hits the interstate, or the plane tips up for liftoff, it's time to tug those laces and pull your paws right out of the **Sweatcave**.

Sock removal is optional, but what's not optional is rubbing your feet against that **little bar thing** that hangs down from the seat in front of you on the bus or airplane to give your stiff, aching soles **The Massage Of Their Life**.

How good does that feel?

So next time, **you're goin' to the grocer**, goin' faster than a roller coaster, remember that breaks like this will, rarely come your way. A-hey, a-hey-hey.

'Cause every day, life seems a little faster, things slip up, **plans turn into disaster**, so ditch your kicks and find a little escape. A-hey, a-hey-hey.

AWESOME!

Getting the eyelash out of your eye

Eyeballs do not want to be touched.

Have you ever put fingers, **algae-filled lake water**, or shampoo in there? Yeah, that gets your eyes screaming in pain pretty quick, doesn't it? Unless you're using baby **No More Tears** shampoo, of course, in which case feel free to lather your eyeballs right on up, no worries.

But seriously, your eyes have their own plumbing system, so they're pretty self-sufficient. Technically they're called tear ducts, but they may as well be called **Eye Toilets** because they just flush your eye out. Nope, no need for any assistance folks, because your Eye Toilets have it all under control. Dust, dirt, tiny little microscopic bugs, flush, flush, flush away.

Your Eye Toilets are great at their job unless, of course, a **rogue eyelash** gets in there. When a rebel lash quietly unhinges itself from the confines of your eyelid and attempts a poorly planned escape to freedom, it's not good. If you're like me and are cursed with **poorly attached eyelashes**, then your lashes just give up and die all the time, flipping down into your eyeball and scratching you right in the cornea. Your

Eye Toilets start flushing madly, but to no avail: That lash is sticking in there tight and it's not budging.

I don't care how many bar fights you've been in or **how many times you've been shot**, you know as well as I do that having an eyelash in your eye is incredibly painful, incredibly annoying, and requires intense focus to get through. You might even have to try one of these eyelash-removing methods:

- **The Pinch and Squeeze Method.** This is where you close your eye tight and pinch 'n' squeeze all your lashes outward, hoping to grab a tiny piece of the rogue lash and pull it out. I recommend doing this one first to see what happens. You miss here and you still have plenty of options.
- **The Eye Blower Method.** Sometimes you need the help of a friend. They can either perform a Surprise Blow to prevent you from defensively closing your eye or they can perform the surgical technique, where you lie down on a bed and hold your eye open while they blow right at the eyelash. That last one takes trust and a very dry, stiff blow. Think **birthday candle blowout**, not warming your hands at the bus stop.
- **The Hard Winker Method.** A solo sport, this is where you just keep winking your eye really, really hard

and hope the lash will eventually pop out. Not a bad technique, though sometimes the act of hard winking just forces that eyelash in there deeper. This one's a gamble.

- **The Eyelid Flapper.** My friend Scott taught me this method when we were kids. You pinch the skin of your eyelid with your fingers and keep popping it in and out real fast until the lash gives up and lets go. This method is gross to look at and comes complete with a marvelously wet and disgusting suction sound.

- **The Wash.** If nothing else works, you can always just splash some water in there. Or, if possible, use one of those dusty eyewash stations hanging out in the back of the wood shop. I've always wanted to see someone use one of those things. They look like they're from a 1950s version of the future.

Look, whatever your strategy, one thing's for sure: You aren't doing **anything** until that eyelash comes out. You might get the job done in five seconds, you might work at it for ten painful minutes, but whatever the case, whatever your style, it sure does feel good when it finally drops out of your eye. Suddenly the sun rises again, the weight is lifted, and your life can get back on the road and just keep on trucking.

AWESOME!

Finally figuring out how your hotel shower works

....

The hotel shower is a **7:00 a.m. Brain Teaser.**

You strip down and peel back the flimsy white curtain to size up the challenger and you find it staring back at you—a clump of shiny dials and spouts with made-up marketing names like Temprol, **Relaxa Shower,** or Aquasomething.

Sometimes that shower tap goes clockwise, sometimes **counterclockwise,** sometimes you have to turn it past cold to get hot, sometimes you pull it toward you to get it going.

And once you eventually get it flowing, you face another challenge: getting it to stop coming out of the bathtub tap and start shooting out of the shower. Your reward for solving this mystery a few minutes later is an ice-cold spray down your naked, shivering body.

Finally figuring out how your hotel shower works is like jumping into the cockpit during an emergency and **landing the plane with no lessons.** You were just woken up and thrown into a tough situation with no instructions, but you managed to figure it out and save the day.

Yes, you're a **clean, freshly scrubbed hero.**

Later on, when you leave the steamy bathroom in your scratchy white hotel towel, be sure to pause for a few moments in the hallway and give detailed advice and directions to all the future showerers of the morning.

They'll thank you for it.

AWESOME!

Talking about how much the meal you're eating at home would cost in a restaurant

There's the new item on the shopping list, the big soup pot or roasting pan you haven't used in a while, and a couple hours of commotion in the kitchen.

But then everyone takes a seat and out pops a **puffy quiche** or simmering curry complete with exotic side dishes. And as drinks are poured, plates are filled, and everyone starts digging into the meal, somebody lobs up the big question.

"Hey, what do you think this would cost in a restaurant?"

And it's a great conversation starter, because now in addition to the feeling of eating good food with friends or family, you get a nice little bonus **Cheapskate High** too.

AWESOME!

When you arrive at your destination just as a great song ends on the radio

There's really nothing like pulling up in the driveway and shutting off the engine just as that final **cymbal crashes** or that wailing guitar solo slowly fades into perfect silence. If you time it just right, you'll miss the start of the commercials, and you'll be rewarded with the song replaying itself in your head all day.

AWESOME!

Saying the same thing a sports commentator says just before they say it

....

Because at that moment you go from being a lazy **potato chips 'n' naps** fan lying on the couch in a crumb-covered pile of sweatpants, bedhead, and B.O. to an insightful sports critic with a sharp eye, quick tongue, and **backup second career**.

AWESOME!

Having really, really good eyesight

AWESOME!

Orange slices at halftime

When I was six years old, my math skills suddenly took a steep tumble, so my parents whisked me off to the eye doctor, who twiddled a bunch of knobs and eventually concluded that this **L'il Squinter** couldn't see the blackboard. Unfortunately, instead of asking me to drink a glass of carrot juice every morning or just sit closer to the front of the class, he wrote me a prescription for some thick **Coke-bottle glasses** and sent me on my way.

Being the only kid in first grade who wore glasses was no fun. I was Four Eyes, Dr. Spectacles, and Blindy, all in one recess.

To make matters worse, they didn't make many glasses frames for kids in those days. At the time, the store had only one pair that fit me—a thick, red plastic set that had to be held around my head with a black elastic band. Yeah, it's true: Not only was I cursed with Blurry Eyes, but I had a side case of Pin Head too. It was embarrassing arriving at school looking like **Steve Urkel**, only without the spunk or sassiness.

Anyway, it didn't take long for those glasses to become the bane of my existence.

I broke them about once a week.

I fell off someone's back in the school yard, crashed into

my sister running around the basement, and got pegged with snowballs on the way home from school. I ran into a fire pole on some **old, dangerous playground equipment**, stepped on them getting out of bed, and left them sitting on couches and chairs around the house. Once I even broke them two days in a row. And it was the same story every time: I sheepishly appeared at dinner with my busted glasses on my face, thick wads of masking tape holding them together, and sat through dinner until my parents very patiently took me back to the same glasses store later that night to buy the same set of red plastic frames again and again and again.

Now, my most painful memory of busting my specs came during a little league soccer game. Almost everyone I knew played soccer as a kid—getting some exercise by joining historical local franchises such as **Chesko's Produce** and **A&R Auto Body, Est. 1956.**

It was in my first and only season, in the middle of a big playoff game, when I unceremoniously took a **well-booted ball** to the middle of my face. My glasses cracked in two. I fell to the ground and started crying, and as the play raced on without a whistle, I slowly got my drippy self together and blindly crawled off the field. I held half my glasses in each hand and wore a **big red circle** on my face from the ball, like someone had set a frying pan on me, accidentally mistaking my round childlike features for a **tightly coiled stove burner.**

Well, I got to the sidelines and was met with bad news. Basically, **the coach wouldn't let me off the field**. See, the problem was that our team was already short players and if I went off we'd be disqualified. Remember—this was the playoffs here. A free pizza party and a round of root beer floats were on the line. Nobody wanted the game to end.

So—completely blind, tears in my eyes, my **bright red well-smacked face** on display for all to see, I stood in the corner of the field for the rest of the game, somehow helping our team avoid disqualification as well as victory.

It was tough.

I remember the only thing that got me through that terrible ordeal was my mom coming over and setting up a lawn chair beside me, popping open a **really, really old Tupperware container**, and giving me all the orange slices I wanted from the halftime stash.

And let me tell you, I loved me some halftime orange slices. They were like sweet liquid energy, filling me with sugar and pep and turbocharging me for the second half.

Now, my showing that day was pathetic and humiliating, I don't deny that. And I'm sad to report that it finally forced me to **hang up the cleats** for good, retiring forever from the game I knew mildly.

But I still remember those orange slices, and my mom generously thiefing the entire container so I could make it through the game. So thanks, Mom.

And thanks, halftime orange slices.

You're both completely . . .

AWESOME!

Putting potato chips
on a sandwich

....

Ever had a friend start buzzing with **The Dating Glow**?

You know, they start seeing someone new and suddenly start walking with a new pep in their step, a new trot in their walk? Maybe they lose five pounds, show up with a new haircut, or start wearing **tight pants**. Or maybe they just smile wider, laugh louder, and blast out a new confidence about themselves.

Being with someone new makes them look and feel better and that's a great thing. That's The Dating Glow.

Now, if you don't mind, let's sharply switch gears and talk about sandwiches——**soggy, squashed, Saran-Wrapped** sandwiches from the bowels of your book bag. Those warm and tired messes look pathetic with sweaty cheese, slimy tomatoes, and warm turkey. Yes, it's a sandwich down on its luck, lacking a bit of confidence, and in desperate need of a glow of some sort.

That's where potato chips come in.

When you crunch up your sandwich with some carefully inserted potato chips, you are injecting a spicy vial of **Grade A Oomph**. Suddenly that pasty gob of bread and meat transforms into a rainbow of crunches and flavors. It's the sandwich equivalent of getting a new hairdo, **wearing something scandalous**, or buzzing with a new vibe.

Now, before we call it a day here, let's chat about something funny about putting chips on a sandwich. Basically, here it is: **Everybody thinks they invented it.** Honestly, I'll be grabbing a quick lunch with a friend from work and he'll just sort of raise his eyebrows at me mysteriously. "Know what I like to do?" he'll ask, squinting a bit and cracking a wry smile. "Put chips on my sandwich, that's what," he'll unveil, a stiff bottom lip, some scrunched eyebrows, and a firm nod echoing the big reveal.

So that's it, ladies and gentleman. Putting potato chips on a sandwich.

You invented it.

We all love it.

AWESOME!

When you didn't play the lottery and your numbers didn't come up

I don't play the lottery very often, but when I do I'm pretty sure I'm going to win. I take pains to ensure all my family's birthdays are evenly covered as I carefully **color in all the bubbles** and then hand my sheet to the convenience store cashier.

Kicking cigarette butts and sucking on a Popsicle while I walk home, my mind wanders off and begins wrestling with difficult questions I assume **plague the rich**: Pool or tennis court? Private jet or yacht? Tall, snooty butler with a thin mustache or fat, clumsy one with a heart of gold?

And I think about whether I'd donate massive chunks of my riches to people who've done small, simple things for me when I was down on my luck. You know, **a million dollar tip** for the coffee shop waitress who calls me Hon, a new mansion for the guy who **slices my cold cuts nice and thin**. I toy with the idea of stashing my cash in a vault and swimming in it like Scrooge McDuck, traveling around the world by unicorn, or possibly just buying the Internet.

My mind entertains these wild dreams because **being a dreamer is great fun**. The thoughts are free, so I enjoy them on my way home, squeezing the ticket in my pocket and then posting it on the fridge so I don't forget the big day.

Yes, this little **Jackpot Fantasy** continues until the numbers are announced. And I don't win. No, I don't even have one number right. I'm not even close. I shouldn't have played. I just threw three bucks away for no reason.

But I guess that's why it's great when I don't play and I check my numbers and sure enough they didn't come up. Now who's laughing?

Me, the three-bucks-richer guy.

AWESOME!

The smell of frying onions and garlic

....

The onion has a long and glorious past. For instance, get this:

- **Ancient Egyptians** used to worship onions. That's right—they believed their spherical shape and concentric rings symbolized eternal life. They also buried their dead with onions, figuring the strong smell might eventually wake them up again.
- In **Ancient Greece** athletes munched on onions because they thought it would lighten the weight of their blood. Remember, this was before no-carb diets.
- **Roman gladiators** were rubbed down with onions to firm up their muscles. Probably helped them slip out of tough bear hugs and sleeper holds too.
- In the **Middle Ages** onions were more valuable than a new jousting sword or decent moat subcontractor. People paid rent with onions and gave them as presents. Doctors prescribed them to move bowels, stifle coughs, and kill headaches. Seriously, imagine a big bag of onions wedged between the eye

drops and skin cream at the drugstore. That's what it was most definitely like back then, I imagine.

Anyway, given the illustrious past of the almighty onion, don't you feel like they don't score enough credit these days? We don't worship them like we used to, but maybe we should. After all, they're still cheap, healthy, and easy to store. Plus they smell delicious **frying in a sizzling glob of butter with minced garlic on top**.

Seriously, when you walk into a house and smell onions and garlic frying, it's a beautiful moment. Partly because they smell great, partly because it means **someone's cooking dinner**, and partly because now you have to solve the mystery of what's cooking. It could be anything, really: pierogies, **sausages**, curry, maybe a stir-fry? The point is that the house smells great and you can't stop salivating.

So next time you're sniffing up that delicious aroma, just remember to stop for a second and think about the onion's proud and noble heritage. Because they've come a long way to be part of your dinner tonight.

And they're happy to be here.

AWESOME!

Nailing a parallel parking attempt on the first try

....

Have you ever driven down a two-lane road with cars parallel parked on both sides and a long line driving in front of you and behind you? I have, and let me tell you: **It's a terrible feeling.**

Most of the time I'd rather drive right by a good parking spot than face **The Audience**, that group of cars driving behind me and strangers beside me that stop to briefly witness the awkward reality show known as **Anyone Else's Parallel Parking Attempt**.

Yeah, my stomach knots up and I lose confidence in my abilities to pull it off. I know the drivers behind me aren't just watching me either. No, they're judging me too, since the quality of my parking has a direct effect on the length of their drive. **If I'm terrible, they wait**, and they know it. They stare at me coldly, locking glances tightly with mine through the rearview mirror, daring me to pull it off.

Then finally I give it a go in one of two ways:

1. **The Driving School Method.** This is where you really don't pay much attention to your car or the space

you have to fit into. You just follow the book—pull up beside the car in front of the spot, put it in reverse, and spin the wheel until you're 45 degrees out into the intersection, and then keep backing up while quickly spinning the wheel the other way really fast. If all went well, you should end up in the spot perfectly. Then again, this method is equivalent to building a bookshelf using the instructions only, without pausing to evaluate your work throughout the process. You might just finish and then stare up at the crooked, unbalanced pile of plywood you just nailed together and wonder what went wrong.

2. **The Advanced Spatial Skills Method.** There's no rhyme or reason to this one. You don't do anything except size up the space and then fiddle and turn your wheel until you fit in. You're just really good at aiming a big piece of metal into a small square hole. You'll go in any which way and then presto magico, finished, simple as that. People who can do this amaze me. I cannot do this.

No, for me it's the Driving School Method all the way. I **have no choice.** Of course, I usually do something wrong, like drive onto the sidewalk or end up a good three feet away from the curb. If I'm three feet away, I try frantically to "drive in" to the spot with an **awkward twelve-point turn,** failing to properly understand the impossibility of this move each time. Eventually I just give up and speed off, fleeing the scene and distancing myself from this horrible embarrassment as quickly as possible.

I guess that's what makes it so great when you actually **do** nail that parallel-parking job on the first try. When you pop into the spot perfectly and tightly, like a battery clicking into a remote control, you get a huge high, a smile reveals itself on your face, and there's an **extra spring in your step**. Cars behind you zoom ahead, happy to keep moving but a little upset you got the spot and they didn't. And once in a while, if you're really lucky, an old guy will barrel-roll out of the nearby barber shop, extend his hand, and say, "Sonny, now **that** was impressive."

AWESOME!

The Perfect Chicken Wing Partner

....

There are two kinds of chicken wings.

First up, there's the **Baby Drumstick**. You know the one. It's a cute, little baby drumstick slathered in wing sauce. It's the photo attachment you'd expect to see on a "We had a baby!" email sent to you from a couple buckets of fried chicken.

Then there are **Flat Pats**. Think of it this way: If Baby Drumsticks are the thick, meaty bicep wings, then Flat Pats are the forearms. Like a forearm, **they've got two bones**, which means you have to tear them apart to get at the tasty meat inside. Don't dismiss Flat Pats, though. Even though they may not have the Baby Drumstick's sex appeal, they come through in the clutch.

Now, some people prefer Baby Drumsticks. Others go for the Flat Pats. Just like some people like their wing sauce mild, some like medium, and some say, "Go suicide or go home."

But people, that's where **The Perfect Wing Partner** comes in. He or she is that special someone who likes **the exact same sauce as you but the exact opposite wing type**. You like medium?

Perfect, so does she. What, you're a Baby Drumstick kind of guy? Great, she's into Flat Pats all the way.

Face it: While you two are chowing down and enjoying your sticky late-night bar food, there's a good chance you'll both glance up at the same time, your sauce-soaked chins glimmering under the neon beer signs, and know, right then, right there, that you've just met your **Perfect Chicken Wing Partner** for life.

AWESOME!

Discovering those little tabs on the side of the aluminum foil box

Put your hand up if you've ever accidentally yanked the **entire roll** of aluminum foil out of the box when you were trying to swipe a small slice.

My brother, if your hand is up right now, you are not alone.

See, I'm a bit clumsy in the kitchen. My oven burners are covered in burnt sauce stains, my sink drains are full of slithery rainbow-colored bits of last night's dinner, and my cupboard of **really, really old Tupperware** looks like a plastic factory exploded.

Add to these issues my apparent love of yanking **entire sheets of aluminum foil** clear out of the box. Honestly, I just give a little tug and out pops the entire roll, hitting the floor and rolling away while laughing its crackly metallic laugh.

Yeah, tell me that's not a pathetic scene: Cut to freeze-frame of tired-looking man in bedhead and sweatpants holding an edge of aluminum foil in one hand and an empty box in the other, then slowly pan down to a floor covered in a thick, shiny snake of crinkled metal.

The only thing that looks worse is the fat, crumpled rolled-back-up roll stuffed in the box when I try to put it together again.

Yes, we've all been there.

But guess what? High tens around the room because there is hope for **People Like Us**. Shockingly, I have recently discovered those little tabs on the side of the aluminum foil box that hold the roll in place! Believe it, food preservation fans, because they truly exist.

Yes, the little tabs on the side of the aluminum foil box can be indented so they **anchor the roll in the box**. Honestly, it's a jaw-dropping discovery—like finding ten bucks in your winter jacket, a secret pocket in your old blazer, or a long-lost son you thought died in a stormy shipwreck.

Now, whenever it was, whenever it is, whenever it will be: How good does it feel when you **first discover** those little tabs yourself? Give it up for a pretty good buzz.

So join me today as we give thanks to that **modern miracle** of the kitchen cupboard.

Those little tabs on the side of the aluminum foil box.

AWESOME!

Your favorite old, comfy T-shirt

Sure, maybe the collar's stretched, **the iron-on's wearing off**, and a moth ate a few holes in the back, but how good does that translucent, tight-fitting second skin feel when you **squeeze into it** and rock it down the street?

AWESOME!

The smell of freshly cut grass

....

Freshly cut grass smells like twilight in the countryside, a football game about to start at the park, or a **sunny Saturday** morning in the suburbs. So whether you're driving down a dusty farm road while the sun sets, stretching before the **whistle blows**, or putting your lawnmower back in the shed after crisscrossing your lot, just stop for a second, tip your head back real far, and take a big whiff, baby.

AWESOME!

A long hug when you really need it

....

Sometimes we all get rattled.

When bad news surprises you, painful memories flash back, or heavy moments turn your stomach to mush, it's great to fall into a warm and comforting pair of big, wide open arms.

Shaking with sobs, dripping with tears, you snort up your runny nose and smear snot across their shoulder as that hug relaxes you and comforts you and helps you get through everything, even for a minute, **even for a moment**.

Maybe there are "It's going to be okay" whispers, some gentle **back rubbing**, or just the quiet silence of knowing that they're not going to let go until you let go first. As their steady arms support you, and the pain washes over you, the hug gives you a warm glow in a shivery moment.

So when you eventually pull back, smile that classic "I'm sorry and thank you" smile, and swipe wet bangs off your forehead, you still might not feel great, but if you're lucky you'll feel a little more

AWESOME!

A good floss after a tough steak

....

How bad was **the first steak** you ever made?

I hope it was better than the **charred shoe** I served for dinner after forty minutes of grilling. Needless to say, I made sure there wasn't anything too raw in the middle there. Nothing too tasty either.

Of course, the worst part about a tough steak is how **it haunts you** for the rest of the evening in the form of tough, stringy bits of beef wedged tightly between your teeth. No matter how hard you twist and turn your tongue, sometimes they don't budge.

That's when you have to bring in the big guns. Yes, that beautiful pack of floss should do the job just fine, thank you very much.

So yank a piece out, snap a piece off, and get down to business. Flecks of **chomped-up beef bits** are released from tight molar deathgrips as your teeth enjoy a tiny moment of sweet relief.

AWESOME!

Dangling your feet in water

Feet need to breathe.

We already mentioned how your **corny paws** are sitting ugly at the bottom of the **You Chain**. Stepped on, squished on, dripping with sweat, they're down low all day getting no love and no respect.

So give them a well-deserved break. Peel those socks off, roll the jeans up, and **flash them ankles**, because it's time to drop your bare, aching feet into some cool water.

So whether it's the gentle lapping on the edge of the dock, soft waves bouncing at the side of the boat, or fountains raining in a public pool, the calming and soothing feeling is good for the soul and good for the soles.

AWESOME!

Salt

....

You're here because of salt.

Honestly, salt's ability to preserve food was a foundation of civilization. People figured they could take their food with them and skipped town with a **lunch bag** to see what was over the hills. Salt affected where roads were built, cities were constructed, and kingdoms flourished.

Get this: During the Roman Empire, caravans of up to forty thousand camels would mosey four hundred miles through the Sahara desert and trade salt for slaves at market. In the 1500s a vast Polish empire rose because of salt mines there but was wiped out when Germans figured out how to make **sea salt** instead. Salt caused wars and ended them, with armies salting the earth before they left to really mess up their enemy's gardens.

Yes, salt was so valuable that it was used as currency. Even the word *salary* was derived from the Latin word *salarium*, which means **money given to soldiers so they could buy salt**.

These days salt costs a dollar and is available everywhere salt is sold. Sure, we've dumped it on **dusty shelves** at the back of the grocery store and preached about its terrible health effects in **fitness magazines**, but let me just say—straight up—that nothing can take away salt's mojo because here we go:

1. **The lady, she brings the iodine.** Health organizations suggest sucking back 150 micrograms of iodine a day to keep fit and have fun. Unless you're eating a lot of seaweed or fresh fish, the best way to pick this up is **iodized salt**. Sadly, the World Health Organization said in 2007 that more than two billion people have iodine deficiency, which results in thick goiters on the neck and stunted physical and mental growth. Not awesome.

2. **Taste the rainbow.** Have you ever tossed salt in a stir-fry of bland vegetables? Buddy, now you're talking. When you add salt, the flavors all have a coming-out party to celebrate. And thanks to salt's powers of preservation, you can enjoy your food long after harvest.

3. **Fights ice real nice.** Those of us from the snowy side of the planet know ice patches on roads and sidewalks are slippery death traps. But kind, giving salt, always there, always ready, busts up those death sheets without hesitation.

4. **It's dirt cheap.** Nobody gets top dollar for salt at the market anymore. Nowadays a handful of warm quarters scores you a year's supply.

5. **Never quits its day job.** Salt has a host of other uses. You gargle with it to help sore throats. Big companies use it to set dyes, keep things dry, and makes soaps and shampoos. Plus, if you've ever had a **giant leech sucking on your neck**, you know that tossing some salt in its face usually gets the job done.

Life sure would be bland without salt. So people, please: If you have a moment, just sit back and remember that salt's come a long way to be here today.

And we've come a long way because of it.

AWESOME!

When you know all the buttons to speed through the automated telephone system

....

If you've called your work voicemail system or local phone company so many times that you know how to jump through all the hoops to get right where you want, then you can **Press 1** for being

AWESOME!

Laughing so hard you make no sound at all

....

!!!

AWESOME!

When you nudge the person snoring next to you and it makes them stop

....

Just tap your elbow in the **rib cage** a bit, maybe pat the belly, or if you're feeling particularly brave, give a kick to the back of the knees while loudly whispering *Shhhhhh* in his ears. If that still doesn't work, it's time to roll him on over, but don't worry: If he wakes up, it will only last a second and he'll never remember it tomorrow.

AWESOME!

The sound of ice cubes cracking in a drink

....

This is the sound of your drink getting colder.

It's the final moment in the sweet series of noises that get you ready for the first sip.

First there's the glass clinking on the countertop, the crack 'n' *phshhhh* of the soda can opening, the *glug-glug-glug* pour, the snapping of the ice cube tray, and the quiet **bloop-bloop** of the cubes dropping in your drink.

These opening acts make way for the big show that is the loud satisfying sound of ice cubes cracking and splitting. As you smile and see your glass frosting up, it's time to give a little swirl and take the first sip.

AWESOME!

Solving the *Wheel of Fortune* puzzle before the people on the show

Sure, most of the time they beat you to the punch. But once in a while you manage to get in there and shout it out before they're done **buying a vowel**. Screaming out the right answer is great because it means you're smarter than three random people on TV. And since at the time you're gorging on a plate of cookies on the couch with your eyelids half-drooped, this is a pretty good feeling.

We'll take it.

AWESOME!

When the guy at the border doesn't ask any questions

··

Crossing the border is stressful.

Long lines, heavy fines, interview questions, **passport inspections**, and through it all you're hoping you don't get an angry customs guy on a power trip. After all, you're completely at his mercy. Unzipping your suitcase, quizzing you on your itinerary, all is fair game.

If you're like me, you get nervous and feel like you might mess up an answer to a question you really do know and sound like you're lying as a result.

"What's the purpose of your trip, sir?"

"Uh . . . what, sorry? Oh, um, I'm just, sorry, I'm just going to Chicago?"

"Please come with me."

That's why nothing beats the **wave-through**. Customs guy, when you deliver that muted two-finger keep-going wave we're loving you lots.

Thanks for letting us in.

AWESOME!

Really, really selling it while barbecuing

....

That thick, smoky **barbecue smell** floats through the yard and everybody starts salivating for dinner.

Yes, sizzling sides of beef and black-burnt wieners are coming right up as the sun's dropping, **the party's hopping**, and your friends are all chilling with ice-cracking drinks on your backyard patio. And if you're in charge of grilling up dinner, then there aren't many things that scream **I'm Serious About This** more than really, really selling it to all your friends. Oh sure, some things come close, such as:

- owning a shiny, oversized nine-piece barbecue tool set and having it folded open on the picnic table
- not leaving the barbecue at any point and even holding on to the handle when the lid is down to make sure nobody attempts to flip burgers when you aren't looking
- wearing a giant apron with your name on it
- asking everybody constant questions at all times such as "Did you say medium or medium-well?" and "You're toasted, you're toasted, you're un-toasted, right?"

Yeah, don't get me wrong, all those things shout **I'm Serious About This** too. But nothing quite screams it like **really, really selling it to the crowd.** You know what I'm talking about if you've ever hammed it up with any of these classic moves:

- "Dog up, I gotta dog up, who wants a dog?!"
- "Come on, Andrew, you're not eating salad, are you? Come on, how many more can I sign you up for? Two at least?"
- *(walking around the deck with raised eyebrows holding a cold cheeseburger on your BBQ flipper and occasionally waggling it in someone's face)*
- "Okay, I got a slightly burnt one. Who likes them nice and crispy? Nice and crispy one here, everybody. Niiiiiice and crispy."

Yes, if you're getting your **barbecue groove** on strong and you're **rocking the sales pitch** long, then kudos to you. Every deck party needs somebody to tell everybody else to eat more burgers. So today we salute you for embracing the job. You sold it. **We bought it.** And now we're all feeling stuffed, bloated, and so completely

AWESOME!

Locking people out of the car and pretending to drive away

There are so many different levels to this classic gag.

There's **Version 1.0**, which involves a carful of people, a gas station bathroom break, the locked door, and the slow-rolling drive away while the victim knocks on the window and pretends not to care. Yes, victims have to avoid giving drivers the frustrated reactions they're looking for here. Folks, this is **Locking People Out Of The Car And Pretending To Drive Away Lite**, a tame version of the gag intended to induce a few giggles without any tense moments. Just some G-rated comic relief for the long drive home. Version 1.0 is the most commonly practiced out there and the officially recommended version by *The Book of Awesome*.

Next up is something a bit more advanced than Version 1.0 but not quite at the level of Version 2.0. We'll call it **Version 1.5**, also known as **The Big Tease**. Now, The Big Tease works as long as the victim leaves his car door open. That open door is critical to pull it off. To execute, the driver simply waits until the victim is approaching the car and then drives away slowly with the door hanging wide open like a big tease. This works fine on small or large cars but is especially effective in vans with sliding doors. You've got that big van door just sitting there wide open and the victim may figure it's worth running and jumping for it. There's really no telling what could happen in this situation. Just remember to be safe out there.

Next comes **Version 2.0**, which involves a carful of people, a gas station bathroom break, the locked door, then a **complete drive away, lap of the gas station, and return after a minute or two**. Big difference here is that Version 2.0 dials up the fear notch a little, instills a bit of bootshake in our helpless victim. When the car comes back, some name calling goes down, but nothing too serious. Still, this one's not recommended for children twelve and under. Let's call it Rated T for Teen.

And then finally there's the granddaddy of them all, the one and only **Version 3.0**. A real cooker, Version 3.0 involves a carful of people, a gas station bathroom break, the locked door, **then a full-out drive away into the sunset without any eventual return**. The victim is left curbside, casually licking an ice cream cone and walking around for a couple minutes, expecting the car to come sweeping around the corner any second now. But no . . . the car never comes back. Unless practiced within walking distance of the victim's house,

Version 3.0 can be devastating. And it's rarely executed and not recommended for obvious reasons: its potential to destroy relationships . . . to destroy relationships . . . forever.

AWESOME!

The sound of rain from inside the tent

Okay, straight up: You know those **big kettle drums** you see in the symphony? The ones being pounded with padded drumsticks by a **bald guy in a tuxedo**? Well, the sound of rain from inside the tent is like living in a kettle drum.

Now, let's be honest. The best thing about the sound of rain from inside the tent is that it means **you're inside the tent**, not outside in a wet T-shirt on your mud-splattered hands and knees, trying to hammer some plastic stakes into the mushy ground. Yes, putting up a tent in the rain is pretty high up there in *The Book of Annoying*, a nonexistent netherlist that also features: Walking into spiderwebs, When you realize you're out of deodorant as you're putting it on, **When someone says the punch line to the joke you're telling**, and Forgetting your umbrella at the restaurant.

The sound of rain from inside the tent feels safe, secure, and comforting. After all, you're out in the elements, safe from the elements. You'll get the **marshmallow roasting sticks** later, you'll build a fire tomorrow, but for now it's time to lie on the **bumpy sleeping bag**, put your hands behind your head, and just enjoy the noise.

AWESOME!

When you arrive at the bus stop just as the bus is coming around the corner

Thin, flimsy plastic sheets propped up on **wobbly rods** shudder in the wind as the **sleet shoots sideways** and you shiver and shake in the dark and lonely bus shelter.

Wrapped in thin gloves and a thick, wet scarf, you stand patiently as your **book-filled backpack** silently jabs your spine and strains your shoulders. Fingers freezing, knees shaking, you wince and hug yourself as you keep looking way up the street, wishing, hoping, praying that you'll please, please see the bus heading right for you.

We've all been there and it's not a pretty scene.

But hey, that's what makes it so great when you hit one of those magic moments where you arrive at the bus stop **just as the bus peels out from around the corner.**

Pupils dilate, eyebrows rise, and a clown-faced smile curls onto your face as you realize you just hit the **Public Transportation Jackpot**.

Yes, in those perfect scenes you're suddenly a **Bus Fleet Fat Cat**, swimming in tickets and tokens, commanding your private army of Sugar Rollers around town to pick you up and drop you off as you see fit. Baby, if you're feeling this buzz, then there's no reason you can't get right into it too—whistling with both pinkies just before it stops or **clapping your hands beside your ear twice** as if you're hailing it for real.

And how perfect is it when this **dream scene** ends with the bus stopping right in front of you, the door swinging open, and the bright round-faced driver flashing you a big toothy smile, a tip of the cap, and a wink as you walk in the door.

AWESOME!

That last crumby triangle in a bag of potato chips

....

Kick-starting a bag of potato chips is pretty much standard—you open with the double-pincer squeeze-and-pop technique, start fishing out the prime, full-bodied chips at the top of the heap, and then work your way down to the half-broken chips in the middle of the bag. A few minutes in you've chomped your way down to the bottom and you might think you're pretty much done. But wait, that's just the beginning.

That's when you get to the best part, that's when you get to the **last crumby triangle** of potato chips wedged right in the corner of the bag. You know what I'm talking about. Usually at this point your lips and face are covered in grease crumbs and your fingers are **neon orange**, coated in a thin film of salty saliva.

That delicious patch of potato powder is all yours, but to get it you have to get a bit dirty:

- First of all, you won't be able to see your fingers down that crinkly, mirrory well, so you have to tilt the bag sideways and size up that crumby triangle for what it's worth. See what you're dealing with here. Commit to a game plan.

- Next, even though your fingers might already be wet at this point, it's best to be safe with the ol' **Thumb & Index Finger Pre-Lick**. Come on, slide them right in and out of your mouth, don't be shy. Remember: The crumbs are in there deep, and your slightly sticky spit-glue will help mine the greasy plunder.

- Next—attack! Wedge your wet thumb and forefinger in there hard, and squeeze until you feel like you've got most of it. Then pull out quick, and in one swift move sweep and drop that last, crumby triangle right onto your tongue, making sure to lick the stubborn remains off your fingers while saying **Mmmm** a lot.

Now, while the **Thumb & Index Corner Pinch** move is gritty and explosive, there is a backup technique that will still get the job done if you don't like to get your hands dirty. Those in the biz know what I'm talking about: the **Dump-Truck Bag-Tilt Maneuver**. This one requires two hands, a gaping mouth, and a 45-degree angle to turn the trick. You can use it alone or in tandem.

But either way, almost entirely composed of salt and artificial flavor, that last crumby triangle packs a **full-flavor**

finishing move, unlike the watered down sip at the end of a soft drink cup, the stump at the bottom of a muffin, or the toothbreaking kernels hiding in that last handful of popcorn.

AWESOME!

Bowling celebrations

....

Because let's be honest: Most people are **pretty stinking awful** at rolling a ball the size and weight of a human head perfectly straight down a sixty-foot lane. There are gutters on both sides, you're slipping in torn-up shoes that have been through **a war and a washing machine**, and every time you go up for a toss you're up onstage with critical eyes piercing holes in your back, watching your every move.

It's pressure, all right.

But that's what makes it so great when you finally pick up a perfect spare or nail a **ten-pin knockdown** in the final frame. That's when it's time for a bowling celebration— ideally featuring several of the following:

1. **The Stage Dance.** Hey, you're up onstage, so why not throw out a couple of moves? Perhaps the famous Hulk Hogan ear cup, the invisible hula hoop, or the fist pump? If all else fails, you can moonwalk back down to your seat. The shoes should help.

2. **The Celebrity.** The paparazzi loves you and you love them back, only without the paparazzi. Smile, wink, and pose for the invisible cameras on your way back to the orange plastic seats.

3. **The All-Business Around-the-World High Five.** This can happen when you have around ten hands to slap. There are just too many hands, so your eyes narrow, your eyebrows crunch, and your tongue fixes itself on your top lip as you focus on nailing every single high five offered to you. You don't miss a slap. Yes, you're all business around the world.

4. **The Overly Exaggerated Jump.** Always a fan favorite. Just watch out for that greasy floor and those skiddy shoes.

5. **The Friendly Stranger.** This is where a casual stranger who has been keeping a passive eye on your game suddenly leaves his lane and jumps into your bowling celebration. The Friendly Stranger can be awkward, but it gives your sweet roll some extra lane cred.

Now, whatever your style, it's important to remember that once you hit down some pins, it's all about the bowling celebration. You can do no wrong at this point, so just relax and do a little dance.

Make a little love.

And get down tonight.

AWESOME!

Slicing open a taped-up box with a set of keys or a pen

....

Don't worry about finding a knife or pair of scissors, because MacGyver's in the house.

AWESOME!

Sitting next to someone good-looking on a plane

Sure, you know how it goes.

Belly gets rounder, **head gets balder**, and that hunch starts poking out the top of your coat. If you're young, don't worry, because those years in the sun and those **years having fun** might hurt your beauty but they can't hurt your pride.

Take it from us.

We're all going to get old one day. So let's just **love the age we've got** and let's not crave the age we're not. Amen, sing it to your mama.

And while we're all smiling and climbing that slow stairway to heaven, golf, and grandkids, I say there's nothing wrong with crossing our fingers and hoping for a **cute seatmate** on that next flight to Florida.

Because Grandpa's got a sideways stare. And Grandma doesn't mind peeking either.

Oh, I know what you're thinking. When we get old, we're the mature, refined, **wise old sages** of society. We're above enjoying the company of some pleasant **eye candy** with a sweet smile for a few hours up in the sky, right?

Speak for yourself, chump.

AWESOME!

When you manage to squeeze out enough toothpaste for one last brush

Say you wake up **Monday morning** and realize you forgot to set your alarm clock. Now not only did you miss some quality snoozetime, but you're late for work to boot. You jump out of bed, **jump on the toilet**, jump in the shower, jump into some clothes, and run to the bathroom to brush your teeth before running out the door.

But then you see it.

That **thin rolled-up toothpaste tube** lying completely empty on your counter, the life squeezed out of it over the past few weeks. Your jaw drops and your memory shoots back . . .

. . . you vividly recall making the first dent in the tube's soft **cylindrical purity**, back when the paste was flowing like water, just itching to flood out. It seemed like it would never end. Over the next few weeks, there were some great moments, like:

- The time you forgot to put the lid on and had to squeeze real hard through a **tiny pinprick hole** in the center of the congealed toothpaste wall the next day.
- The first time you had to roll it up, coiling the thick, once-mighty **toothpaste anaconda** into a

tightly wound fraction of itself. This was foreshadowing, but the paste kept flowing so you thought nothing of it.

- The time you actually thought you were out of toothpaste but managed to unroll it and slide it real hard across the edge of your bathroom counter, completely coaxing all the minty green molecules up to the front door.

You smile slightly at foggy memories of better days, before your brain quickly jerks you forward to the present.

Which is right now.

When you're late for work.

You stare into your empty tube of toothpaste, **glance quickly at your watch**, and decide to just go for it, one last time.

You grab your brush, grit your teeth, and squeeze your thumb and forefinger together as hard as you can, right on the head of the tube. You squeeze and squeeze and squeeze and squeeze, your thumb pounding, **your brow pulsing**, your brush pleading . . .

. . . until it finally comes: that very last, very weak, **very small dot of toothpaste**, peeking its head out the toothpaste tube tip just in time for you to swipe it with your brush, swish it around your mouth, and spit it out.

AWESOME!

Using Q-tips the way you're not supposed to use them

Yes, I'm talking about **rubbing and twisting** that cottony Q-tip tip right inside your ear canal. Get it in there deep, where it doesn't belong, because it's like an amazing, satisfying **inner-ear massage**.

Also, the more **dark, waxy, and disgusting** the Q-tip is when you're done, the more satisfying it is, am I right? Because then on top of the inner-ear massage, you get a killer "Whoa, that just came out of me . . ." high too. For those keeping track at home, that's two highs for the price of one. **Not a bad deal!**

Now, I know what you're thinking: How could we possibly advocate doing something so terribly dangerous like pushing a hard, pointy object against your fragile ear drum? I mean, the box itself says right on it: "**Do not insert swab into ear canal.** Entering the ear canal could cause injury."

But come on, we all do it. And we know we probably shouldn't. It's dangerous and unnecessary and risky and illegal and against all common sense.

But it feels so good.

AWESOME!

Watching *The Price Is Right* when you're at home sick

....

At an early age, it is possible to learn the price of life through *The Price Is Right*.

How many eight-year-olds know a can of chickpeas costs eighty-nine cents? How many twelve-year-olds can rattle off the features of a new solid oak armoire? And how many fourteen-year-olds can estimate the value of an ice cream maker, new speedboat, set of maracas, and trip to Puerto Rico?

Well, I'll tell you who, man: **any kid with the flu.**

See, *The Price Is Right* is great when you're sick because it comes on at 11:00 a.m., which is about the time your enthusiasm for missing school is sort of deflating into a boring day on the couch with a stomachache. By midmorning, whoever is taking care of you has either headed upstairs or thrown a blanket on you and **gone grocery shopping**. You feel too sick to do much of anything, so you just lie on the couch and flip channels endlessly, trying to understand why there's nothing good on TV.

Then finally, as you've finished counting cracks in the ceiling, tried and failed to **legally nap** several times, and mindlessly gobbled down a pack of saltines, the clock strikes 11:00 a.m. and it's time for the show.

That's when the music starts kicking, **the lights start flashing**, and it's time to come on down. Because it's *The Price Is Right*, baby. So sing it with me and let's get in the game. It's just such a great time.

And, you know, I think it really helps that everybody on *The Price Is Right* is just so happy—people are running and jumping, laughing and screaming, and they're all wearing homemade T-shirts to boot. **Basically, they feel the exact opposite of how you feel and it's sort of contagious.**

The Price Is Right is one massive climax of games, prizes, and tuna fish ads. But you find yourself cheering along and guessing the price of that leather ottoman, yelling for the big wheel to stop on $1.00, and crossing your fingers for the announcer to unveil a game of Plinko or, yes . . . a new car!

And yeah, I know it's different now, but come on, for how many years did *The Price Is Right* represent some solid, rocklike consistency in this mad, mad, mad, mad world? There was Rod Roddy's sequined blazer, the wildly panning camera looking for the next contestant, Bob Barker's **skinny microphone**, and shots of the family in the audience madly screaming advice to help our hapless contestant win a four-piece bedroom set.

It just never changed.

And so whether you were six with the chicken pox, nine with the flu, twelve with a broken arm, or fifteen with menstrual cramps, you could count on sixty solid minutes with the company of that old seventies set, **lots of one-dollar bets**, and advice to neuter your pet, all crunched into the best sick-day game show yet!

AWESOME!

That one square in the waffle that's the most loaded with butter and syrup

Oh, you know the one.

It's full to the brim with a melty smear of butter and drenched in a puddle of thick syrup.

Good move saving it for last.

AWESOME!

Rain hair

You know when you get caught in the rain and your fabulous hairdo turns into a wet, frizzy mess? Well, I say that's a good thing. Because hear me out.

Let's talk about how much time, money, and effort we put into the managing and upkeep of our golden locks of **dead skin cells**. How about a lot? Now, don't get me wrong, I play the game too. I wash my hair, condition it up, gel it up, shake it up. I prepare it for the day and check in periodically to see how it's doing. Any rogue locks, fallen bangs? What's new in the slowly-going-bald corners? How's that **back-of-the-neck beard** coming in this month? I spend too much time on it and my hair still looks like a squirrel that's been run over on the highway for a few weeks.

Our pals over at Wikipedia make hair sound like **the sun** or **fresh water**, saying in their snooty tone that head hair has "gained an important significance in nearly all present societies as well as any given historical period throughout the world." But then again, those lovable eggheads can make anything sound pretty serious. It's just hair, after all.

I say maybe the army got it right when they instituted crew cuts after World War I trench warfare gave everyone **lice and fleas**. Maybe there's something to be said about the no-maintenance plan, the low-maintenance plan, or the no plan at all. Because whenever I walk by someone with hair just flying everywhere, all unkempt and full of knots, dirty dreads, and **dead leaves**, I get jealous for a second. Think of the free time they have! I mean sure, they stick out, but what if we all got in the game? Then maybe everyone's garden would look immaculate, gyms would get really crowded, and libraries would run out of books. We'd just have to put up with all these shaggy, scraggly Sasquatches walking around, that's all.

And that's what I kind of like about rain hair. It's a temporary escape from the **Hair Prison** we live in. When everyone shows up at the movies or mall with wet and frizzy flyaways, hair matted to their foreheads, and **hair spray dripping and stinging their eyes**, it's like, yeah, we all look like a mess.

But that rain sure does wash away expectations too.

AWESOME!

Neighbors with pools

....

Hey there, neighbor. Thanks a lot for paying for that massive, expensive pool! Great job installing it, heating it, chlorinating it, vacuuming it, and skimming it. You sure it's cool if I take you up on that offer to swing by for a quick dip?

AWESOME!

When you actually remember the name of someone you met earlier at the party

I have a problem.

Within seconds of meeting somebody I completely forget their name.

Sure, I introduce myself, **shake hands**, and jump right into conversation, but I can't fully concentrate because I realize their name has immediately disappeared from my memory. Cursing myself, I silently scan my frontal lobe, but my pink and lumpy mush is **bright white** and empty.

So I smile and nod along, but inside I'm frustrated. And it's even worse when they use my name right away. "So Neil, where you from?" they'll ask innocently, but I'm too busy combing through cobweb-covered spare parts in **Skull Factory** to properly answer them. My eye contact drifts and I get distracted and fidgety.

It's at these desperate times that I try one of the three **Name-Teasing Techniques** I've learned over the years:

1. **The Take Two**. A friend joins my side at the party and I say to the Mystery Man, "Oh, have you met

Chad?" hoping that Chad will put his hand out and lean in with a "Nice to meet you! Sorry, what was your name?" If Chad nails it, I give him a high five later. If he doesn't, I throw a cup of punch in his face so he gets it right next time.

2. **Spell Check.** If I don't remember their name, but I think it was long or complicated, then I ask them to spell it for me. If they say P-a-r-d-e-e-p, then I'm all aces, if they say P-a-m, then I'm an idiot. High risk, high reward.

3. **The Anecdote Wait.** This is an absolutely terrible move that I use all the time. It involves waiting until they finally tell an anecdote where they refer to themselves by their first name. For example: "So my ex-boyfriend finally said, 'Catherine, it's either me or that cat' . . . and I picked the cat!" With an anecdote like that, you just found out her name is Catherine so you're good to start using it. Also, no cat jokes.

Sure, these techniques look easy, but the truth is that they're awkward and embarrassing to use with no guaranteed results. Let's be honest, it's much more satisfying to actually remember and drop their name right at the beginning of a sentence with confidence, like you've been old friends for years.

Then they'll look back at you with beaming eyes and a bright smile that shows you two are getting to know each other. Hey, maybe you'll see each other again, maybe you'll become friends, maybe you'll do business, maybe you'll start dating.

All because you remembered their name at the party.

Nice move, you.

AWESOME!

Somebody flashing their high beams at you to warn you about the cops

....

Tired and groggy, you're driving late at night, whipping down side streets and back paths to get home a bit faster, your eyelids drooping, your body achy and sore. Occasionally there are headlights in the opposite direction, **blurry whiz-by streaks** of bright white——shift workers, truck drivers, and party animals all riding the lonely roads, trying to get somewhere quick.

Then suddenly an approaching car **flashes its high beams** at you. Blinded, you sit up, awake and alert, checking all your mirrors, slowing the car down. What's going on, you wonder, until a few seconds later when you pass a cop car with its lights off, sitting on the side of the road, a patient and silent predator waiting for its prey.

"Thank you," you whisper under your breath as you drive by under the speed limit. "Thank you, thank you, thank you."

Part of what makes this great is the fact that **the flasher** is going the opposite way and can't really get the favor returned. You don't know him or her, him or her don't know you, but they threw the favor out there, a warm passing smile on a dark drive, no payback required or expected. It's **The Late-Night Driver's Pact**, a rebellious fight-tha-police stance that helps everyone out in the pocketbook a bit.

So you smile as you drive on, and when you see another car heading in the opposite direction, you know what to do.

Flash them high beams, sister. Flash them bright and light up the night.

AWESOME!

The Man Couch

The Man Couch is any couch **conveniently located near the change rooms in a women's clothing store.**

You can tell which one's The Man Couch because it's generally covered in man. Most are either text messaging, **illegally napping**, or staring straight ahead, jaws dropped, pupils dilated, completely zoned out, their arms full of purses and bags from other stores.

Now, The Man Couch really is good for everybody:

For **women**, it gives them a convenient place to find their male shopping companion. There they are, right outside the change room! This is much better than having to track them down in the **magazine section** of the bookstore or in the line for fries at the food court. Also, it's great knowing your purse is safe and there's an opinion available if you want it.

For guys, The Man Couch is a place of solace and comfort. Its giving cushions provide a quiet reprieve from the unrelenting **Day of Shopping**. Surrounding guys are fellow travelers with worn-weary eyes telling cautionary tales of **Seven-Sweater Fashion Shows** and **Lineups for Hemming**. Yeah, it's a tired, quiet gang sitting there in the couch hostel at the back of the store.

So thank you, Man Couch. Without you our calves would be burning **even more**, our boyfriends would be at the **record store**, and we'd all be **sitting on the floor**.

The Man Couch, ladies and gentlemen!

AWESOME!

The shampoo head massage you sometimes get at the hairdresser

Close your eyes, dip your head in the sink, and relax as that warm shower gets sprayed all over your scalp. Then smile softly as the hairdresser tenderly rubs and massages your head with shampoo and conditioner. Relax, unwind, and detensify as you slowly climax toward **Total Scalp Actualization**.

AWESOME!

Finding the TV remote after looking forever

....

Look, there it is, wedged way down in the couch cushions this whole time.

AWESOME!

Adrenaline

....

Did you know you have two yellow **nine-volt-battery-sized** adrenal glands in your body, just chilling out, maxin' and relaxin' all cool on top of your kidneys? Someone told me this and I checked it out. Turns out it's true.

It seems as though your adrenal glands are kind of like those **British Royal Guards** with the big black fuzzy hats who stand like statues in front of Buckingham Palace. They just stand there quietly, not doing much really, just enjoying the **brown slippery beach** that is your kidneys.

However, if anything startling should happen that requires your attention—like you're about to give a speech at a wedding, **a twig cracks outside your tent**, or your doorbell rings in the middle of the night—then they leap into action, jumping out of their peaceful slumber to squeeze a big dose of adrenaline right into your body, pumping you up and turning you into a primal warrior-like version of yourself.

When tension runs high and adrenaline is secreted into your body, some crazy things can happen, which is sometimes called the **fight-or-flight** response:

- **Your heart rate increases.** And specifically, your body starts sending blood to all your big muscles and diverts it away from "non-critical" parts of your body like your brain, immune system, and stomach. I guess someone figured you could digest the sandwich after you killed the bear.

- **Your pupils dilate and you get tunnel vision.** Quite literally, adrenaline also reduces your peripheral vision, which together with your big, wide pupils helps you focus on what lies ahead. You can't quite see through walls, but if a crow is diving at your eyes you might be able to swat it away better.
- **Your body gets ready to boot it.** In addition to the rising heart rate, your body starts turning piles of inner goo into sugar and fills you with energy. You might not feel pain as easily, so the raspberry bushes that shred your legs when you're running out of the forest won't slow you down.

What's also great about adrenaline is that you don't have to control it. It kicks into high gear when it figures you need a boost. I think it's kind of cool knowing that your body will help you out when you need it most. **Punch me in the face** and suddenly my internal British Royal Guard tosses away his fuzzy black cap, cracks his neck, and rolls up his sleeves.

And really, isn't it that little dose of adrenaline that helps you do a better job when you need it most? It's a **natural upper**, helping you nail the big speech, ace the final exam, or perhaps flee both of those scenes.

There's a reason some people become **adrenaline junkies**. The boost you get from your adrenal glands waking up and getting out of bed is intoxicating. Sure, it fuzzes up your thinking and sends your intestines on sabbatical, but it pumps you up.

So remember: When something important in your life is about to happen, you can count on your good pal adrenaline to be there cheering you on and helping you fight the good fight.

AWESOME!

Getting a trucker to blow his horn

Truckers have the best horns.

Those things mean business. They're loud and thundering and slap you in the face. See, when a hatchback lets out an itty-bitty bee-beep telling you the light turned green, it sounds like a seagull telling other seagulls, **Hey, there's a guy tossing crusts over here.** When a trucker does the same thing, it's a full-on roar, the sound a tugboat would make if it was about to crash into a lighthouse.

Sometimes, when you're driving down the highway, the hours keep going and going and going. Rod Stewart, Meat Loaf, and the whole mix tape gets stale, conversation dies down, and it's just a blur of **interstate walls and rest station signs** out the window. For kids without distractions it can seem like days back there, strapped right in and sitting in a numbing silence broken up only by potholes and passing motorcycles.

That's why getting a trucker to blow his horn is great. It's a laugh and a fun, little interactive break from highway monotony. Plus, it's a time passer, because you have to get the driver to sort of ease up beside the truck first, which isn't always easy. It's a secret moment on wheels, **a honkin' highway holler**, and some good old-fashioned bonding in the fast lane.

So let's give thanks to truckers. For not taking life too seriously, for indulging our simple pleasures, and for rocking that blasting air horn in a special moment we like to call

AWESOME!

When there's leftover cake in the office kitchen

....

Ever had a birthday party in the office?

If you have, you know that it's usually celebrated with a **streamer-covered cubicle**, a signed birthday card, and a mid-afternoon cake. And while everyone says they don't want that cake, let's be honest: After you start including it in your diet two to three times a week, you **can't stop jonesing for that two o'clock sugar rush**.

Of course, after the parties happen the partially eaten leftovers find their way to the office kitchen. To get in on the game you'll need to follow these **Top Four Tips for Scoring Leftover Office Cake**:

1. **Keep extra plastic forks and paper plates at your desks.** Because how many times do you happen upon a partially devoured cake, only to notice that there's nothing to eat it with? Put up your icing-smeared hand if you've ever dug into that cake anyway. Yeah, I'm talking about slicing the cake with a coffee stirrer, using a piece of paper from the printer as your plate, and tossing it back like a crumbly

Jell-O shooter. It's not pretty and it's sort of crossing the line between **Friendly Coworker** and **Office Raccoon**. I say don't be the raccoon. Keep cutlery at your desk.

2. **Do your cubicle rounds.** On your way into work in the morning, make sure you do your cubicle rounds. You know, just checking out if anybody's desk is decorated for their birthday. If you spot one, it's a good omen of cake to come.

3. **Buddy up.** When they find cake, they tell you. When you find cake, you tell them. There's always enough to go around, so why not double your odds of scoring an icing flower? You know you have a great Cake Buddy when you find a piece of cake covered with a napkin sitting on your desk when you get back from a meeting. Now, that's service. Make sure to thank them with a corner slice next time.

4. **Know the peak times.** Office birthday parties nearly always happen in the afternoon because this allows someone to run out and grab a cake at lunch. So make sure you're ready and aware of those mid-afternoon fake meetings that turn into birthday parties. Also, it doesn't hurt to swing by the kitchen at 2:30 p.m. to see what's cooking, if you catch my drift.

Now, these are all great methods for how to score leftover cake from the office kitchen, but what happens if you're invited to the actual office birthday party itself? Well, don't worry, we've got you covered with one big rule: **If you're at the party, don't be the Table Setter, Servant, or Salesman.** You must make a strong effort to avoid these three dreaded office party tasks because they will delay your cake eating:

- **The Table Setter** is the guy assigned to finding plastic forks, paper plates, and drink cups at the last minute. It's no fun leaving the party to run around and beg for Styrofoam. Best show up a bit late or mingle undetected in the back.
- **The Servant** ends up closest to the cake . . . just in time to cut it for everyone! Yeah, now you're stuck trying to split up those much-too-thin paper plates, put a fork on each one, and slice that cake up. It's a lot of pressure being the Servant, because everybody is crowding around you and yelling things like "No, no, no, **half** that size!" And it can all happen so fast that you don't even realize you're the Servant until you find yourself in the bathroom twenty minutes later awkwardly washing the cake knife with cold water and paper towels.
- **The Salesman** takes the cut pieces of cake and walks around the room, selling them to everybody. If you

get the job, your best move is simply asking "Who doesn't have a piece yet?" and then waggling the cake in people's faces till they take it off your hands.

So that's it, ladies and gentlemen. Now that you've got it down, get ready for some sugar comas because you're entering a world of all cake all the time.

And it will be glorious.

AWESOME!

Hanging your hand out the car window

....

On a warm, sunny day in a car with the window open and your hair whipping around everywhere, what's better than letting your hand slip safely out the window and letting it **wildly roller-coaster** against the wind?

You know how it is: That speeding car creates a strong and forceful **wind pocket** that's fun to ride, and as you let it slip and slide across your fingers, you can kind of close your eyes and pretend you're flying.

AWESOME!

Getting served breakfast in bed

It's **Mother's Day** and your kids wake you up with a plate of cold toast, runny eggs, and a short glass of lukewarm OJ. Sure, it may not be the best-tasting meal in the world, and yeah, you might spill crumbs on your sheets, but don't tell me getting served breakfast in bed isn't the greatest.

I mean, there you were just sleeping and someone else said, "Let's go downstairs and cook up our best possible meal, toss it on a tray, and bring it upstairs and serve it to you." Yes, serve it to you! Cook it up and set it up and serve it to you. I have to say you're pretty lucky if this happens to you.

Breakfast in bed can also help accomplish the exotic **get up and eat up and get back down** move, a brilliant Saturday or Sunday feat that involves filling your belly with breakfast and then immediately crashing back into a **post-fiesta siesta**. It's a great feeling hitting the sheets and flipping the pillow on that full stomach. And who knows? Maybe there's lunch in bed just waiting for you on the other side of those sleepy dreams. No, honestly, it's a good question: Has anyone ever actually scored lunch in bed? If so, I'm pretty sure you win the **World's Greatest Day Ever** contest.

Now, the **Trump Card** for turning a good breakfast in bed into a great one is when it includes one or more of the following:

- one of those tiny miniature glass bottles of ketchup or jam
- a homemade greeting card wishing you a Happy Mother's Day or Happy Birthday
- a breakfast dessert of any kind
- butter painstakingly carved into a perfect cube or sphere
- cute restaurant-style folded-up napkins

Let's be honest, people. We sure do love eating. **We sure do love sleeping.** And breakfast in bed is the closest we get to combining both at the same time. You know what we think of that.

Say it with me now.

AWESOME!

Finally clipping your fingernails after you've been meaning to do it all week

....

Long fingernails consume me like a drug.

Sometimes while **buttoning my shirt**, I look down and notice my nails have grown a little bit. So I keep buttoning but silently pledge to trim them at night after I get home.

Of course, after work I generally can't find the nail clipper, so I instead choose to fall asleep on the couch at 8:30 p.m. after scarfing a handful of nachos for dinner. Then I wake up at three in the morning, walk to bed with a **crink in my neck**, and sleep a few more hours until the alarm buzzes, at which point I'll groggily stumble around my place **buttoning up my shirt**, silently pledging again to cut my fingernails later that night.

This will continue day after day until I've grown a **freakishly large set of claws** that makes me look like an eagle. Yes, my nails get worse and worse until **the moment** comes when I can no longer live with myself and finally snap. That's when I run to the drugstore and buy a new set of clippers and maddeningly chop my nails off in a fit of rage.

Hey, finally pulling off that **big, long-awaited clip** is great because it's not a trim, it's a full-on shear. You get the clipper right in the grooves, cutting them bit by bit until the big sharp shards lie in a crumpled napkin beside you. And you sort of feel a little buzz of pride, relief, and cleanliness—like you just gutted a fish, snipped off your **college dreadlocks**, or sold all the dusty junk from your basement in a yard sale.

Smiling with pride as you inspect your new **tingly, hypersensitive** fingertips, you pause for a second and wonder if the world's ready for this whole new you.

AWESOME!

Coming home after a long day to the smell of someone cooking dinner

....

Brain boggled, pants greasy, heels too high, tie too tight?

Can you feel your heartbeat in your temples? Does your bad breath taste like paint? Is your carpal tunnel syndroming? Because if so, Office Joe, then maybe it's been a long day. Maybe you stapled too many **expense reports**, got buried under too much homework, or had an inky run-in with a **photocopier** at the end of the day without an Unjammer Man around.

But you scrape by, you scrape home, you scrape up to the front door—**tired and sore, aching from war**—as the sun sets behind you, the traffic jams behind you, and your stomach rumbles inside you. That bagel you scarfed six hours ago is a distant memory, but you're much too exhausted to do anything besides dial for pizza.

And that's what makes it so great when you pop open your door and catch a hot whiff of **something sizzling** in the kitchen. Even though your clogged-up, toner-infused brain can barely soak up anything, you somehow manage to piece things together: "Dinner me eat. Food yes now."

And suddenly there is life.

Your lips slowly curl at the corners, your **nose sniffs at the nostrils**, and your eyes flash a quick cartoonish sparkle with a faint **ding** heard somewhere in the background. You've got new energy, so you kick off your shoes, peel off those sweaty socks, and let the saliva start to flow for some tasty eats cooked up **hot and fresh** by someone you love.

AWESOME!

Big crowds enjoying big fireworks

Fire trickles and drips across the sky, old folks huddle and cuddle and babies cry, teenagers squeeze sweaty palms and look up, up way high. Because light fills the night, **kabooms bang in the air**, conversations stop, jaws drop, we all crane our necks up and stare. Yes, when those fireworks erupt, when they splash in the dark, **when those bright waterfalls drip down into our park**, we all ooh and ahh at them big beautiful sparks.

AWESOME!

Sleeping with one leg under the covers and one leg out

Home temperature is important.

Head in the freezer, hands in the oven, whatever your move, just make it. Pick a temp, baby, then bake it. Pump up the thermostat, bang on the rad, or crank up the air. If you're hot, ditch the **sweatpants**, if you're cold, slip on slippers.

Home temperature is important.

If you're not comfortable, you just won't be happy. Roommates want it hotter, spouses want it cooler, and you may want it *jusssssssssst* right, so you'll need to **tweak dials** and add layers until you figure it out.

And eventually you will. And you'll think everything is great. And everything will be great.

Until it comes.

Bedtime.

Yes, before you flick out the lights and slip into golden slumbers, you must first guess your Sleep Comfort Zone (SCZ or "See-Zee" for short). And See-Zees ain't easy. If you've ever woken up with the shivers or the sweats, then you added too many blankets or slept **too nude**.

If you're on your own, there are ceiling fans, heating vents, and your **general sweatiness** to consider. If you're with a pet or a partner, you've got double the hot-breath factor and a lot more sweaty legs under the covers.

If you're like me, then your eyes might **blink open** in the middle of the night as you realize you're uncomfortable. And if this happens, then just toss one leg out of the covers and one leg under them.

Also known as the **Toe Vent**.

AWESOME!

Building a stack of pancakes that looks just like the front of the box

It's no joke and it takes teamwork, timing, and trust, but building a stack of pancakes that looks just like the front of the box can be one of the **most rewarding breakfast experiences of your life**. Here's how you can make the magic happen:

1. **Assemble a team.** You'll need a Cook, Condimenter, and Table Setter. The Cook should be an early riser and self-starter, with the skill and confidence to cook for a group as well as a basic understanding of what a circle looks like. Your Condimenter needs to understand the value of real butter and decent maple syrup and know where to find it. A driver's license is necessary here. And lastly, there's the Table Setter. Prior experience is mandatory. Also a plus is the ability to fold napkins into nice triangles.

2. **Night-before prep work.** Yes, the show begins the night before. The Condimenter needs to make sure all the key ingredients are in the house. Is there enough powder in the pancake box? Is the tap

water running okay? How about the syrup and butter? If necessary, make a list and go to the store before it closes. We don't want to find out in the morning that something's missing. Nobody will sleep well not knowing.

3. **Rest up.** It doesn't matter what time you go to sleep. Just make sure you squeeze enough solid hours of golden slumbers in there to power up the juices and get the engine revving the next morning. Remember: Groggy kitchen work is sloppy kitchen work. Nobody likes an oblong pancake.

4. **Wake up and get down to pancakes.** Showtime! Now it's the Cook's time to shine. This job is not for the weak-minded. The Cook must first set the oven to a low temperature because that's going to be the holding bay until we have a full stack. This is a slow-building crescendo toward a massive stack of pancakes. Let's not forget that. Once we've got the oven set low, the Cook starts doing their thing— tying their hair into a bandana, getting the frying pan warmed up, mixing the batter. There can be no breaks until the full stack of pancakes is cooked, kept warm, and ready to serve. The Table Setter is busy here too, pulling out silverware, laying out plates, folding napkins. And rounding out this majestic circus-like performance is the Condimenter,

busy pouring juice and jigsawing perfect squares of butter.

Team, **remember what we're playing for here**: a towering stack of hot, fluffy pancakes drizzled with sweet, slow-moving syrup, delicately topped with a thick, perfectly melting square of butter.

Yes, it takes some time. Yes, it takes real effort. Yes, you will require a solid lineup of team players who never take their eyes off the end goal. But what could be more fun on a weekend morning than creating your very own stack of pancakes that looks just like the front of the box?

(Hint: Nothing.)

AWESOME!

When your sneeze stalls for a second and then suddenly comes booming out

....

Your head is a machine.

Honestly, just face it: Your face and scalp are really just **oily gift wrap** over the giant, whirring **Skull Factory** running full throttle inside your coconut. Just think about what's going on up there.

First you've got sound waves constantly navigating your twisty, waxy ear canals like **Luke Skywalker** weaving through Death Star trenches. Then there's your nose on permanent high-sniff alert, searching out gas leaks in the basement, fresh croissants at the bakery, or **coffee aisles in the grocery store**. And we can't forget your mouth and nose forever dancing together in the majestic **art of breathing**.

But wait, that's not all. On top of these rickety assembly lines of important Head Business, you've got blood swirling around, mucus dripping all over the place, and neurons firing and bouncing off walls like a million never-ending games of **Pong**.

Skull Factory's a busy place, folks. The line keeps moving every day, every night, every year, forever.

Given how much is going on, it's no wonder the **gears get**

gummed up once in a while. Rogue lashes jam your sockets, Popsicles give you brain freeze, and sneezes stall in your **clogged-up noggin** just as they're trying to escape.

And you know what that feels like.

Face frozen in an **awkward crunch**, you stare at the ceiling and hold your hand up to your friend, silently pleading with the factory foreman to please, please just let it out. One eye popped open, the other squeezed shut, you clench your cheeks, bend your mouth into a triangle, and feel the lost sneeze pinball around your skull.

And then **BOOOOOM!**

Oh mama, how good does it feel when that sneeze finally comes screaming out?

Really, that sweet release is like someone yanking a **red-hot, twisted wrench** out of your grinding, crunched-up head-gears and letting all the oily parts start quietly purring again.

AWESOME!

Wordless apologies

Tension fills the room and **black clouds** linger by the ceiling fan. Dinner was late, bills piled up, nobody called home.

Now you're steaming in front of the TV while they're crying softly in the bedroom upstairs. The stalemate burns quietly until they come down, enter the room slowly, grab your shirt sleeves, and look right at you with warm, moist eyes while starting to give you a soft, smiling apology.

But you see them coming and your stomach churns with a **wave of regret**, so before they even get it out, you interrupt with a head shake and a hug.

AWESOME!

The smell and sound of a campfire

....

Slicing a dead tree, tossing it on a pile of dirt, and setting it on fire is pure joy.

As that **dry, withered stump** slowly releases years and years of energy soaked up from the sun, the air, and the **ground around** it, out come bright lights, whispering hisses, sizzling pops, and the thick intoxicating smell of **Musky Smoke 'n' Pine Needles**.

You can close your eyes and let your eyelids paint **yellow and orange kaleidoscopes** as the heat washes over you, rosying up your cheeks and giving you that nice, warm **Hotface Effect**. In that cold, dark forest, on that cold, dark log bench, beside the cold, dark lake, your ears and nose perk up as you focus on every little sound and smell around you.

AWESOME!

When your suitcase tumbles down the luggage chute first after a long flight

My friends have theories.

"If you're the first person to check in for the flight you're pretty much done for," my friend Chad will begin as our plane begins its slow descent. "Your suitcase is first in the plane and gets buried under everyone else's golf clubs, **guitar cases**, and bird cages."

"No, no, no, it's not like that at all," Mike will counter, sipping his diet cola and shaking his head slowly. "If you're last to check in, you're last one out. Fair is fair. Unless you're in **first class** or have a special membership tag, they observe the rules of **suitcase etiquette**. These are big companies. They have standards."

"You're both wrong," I'll sigh with the pompous air of a frustrated **airline CEO**. "I wish there was a science to it, but honestly the system's in shambles. Look, if you were tossing backbreaking luggage in the **bowels of an airport** all day, do you think you'd follow the rules of 'suitcase etiquette'? No, you just grab bags randomly. It's all completely random. Nobody knows what's coming out."

The conversation reaching a stalemate, we all shrug and look away from one another. Mike glances out the window at the bright lights below and Chad flips passively through an in-flight magazine article about **resort swimming pools with interesting shapes**.

Tired and sore, we land, clear customs, and make our way to the luggage belt. Away from the theories and debate, one thing becomes extremely clear: It sure feels great when your suitcase tumbles down the luggage chute first.

If this happens, part the **anxious crowd**, grab your bag, and shuffle outside to get on your way. Smile a big smile because you just won the suitcase jackpot.

AWESOME!

Peeling off your wet bathing suit and putting on warm clothes after swimming for a long time

....

Nipples freeze, **goosebumps rise**, and you get a shaky case of the shivers.

Yes, when you jump out of the pool after a long swim, the wind just whips by and chills you to the **bone marrow**. For a moment you're frozen in that drippy no-man's-land between warm soothing pool water and dry puffy beach towel. Hair matted to your ears, cold water trickling down your legs, you run across the grass or up the patio stones into the warm embrace of a towel. Quickly you dry your hair and face, scrub your arms and legs, and then wrap it around you in the classic **Caped Crusader Huddled On A Skyscraper Rooftop** pose.

And sure, you love the feeling of warming up again, but there's just one nagging problem: that cold, wet bathing suit clinging damply to your rear end. Icy drops drip down your legs until you finally go inside, head to the bathroom, and get the job done in three easy steps:

- **Step 1: Slow Peelin'.** Bikini rockers, you're done in a jiffy, untying the top and dropping your bottoms into a tiny inside-out mess of wet spandex on the floor. If you're rocking trunks, just peel them down your dry legs, even if they stick and clump awkwardly until you eventually kick them off in a fit of rage.

- **Step 2: Finish the job.** Clammy butt cheeks hanging coldly under the blowing bathroom vent, you grab your towel and complete the dry, this time with intense focus on your nether regions. When you're sure the chilly dampness is finally gone, it's time for heaven.

- **Step 3: Heaven.** Slip on the soft cotton and slide up your warm, dry pants. Because you were so cold it kind of feels like wearing underwear just out of the dryer. You're loving every minute of it and hurry back to hit the deck for a burger or a beer.

You're back, baby.
AWESOME!

Bedhead all day long

Sure, anybody can wake up with some **serious bedhead**.

Tangled dreads, pillow-dented part, static-flared bangs—whatever you got, we'll take it. Much like rain hair, bedhead is your temporary ticket to **Cowlick Country**, a place where looks just don't matter. It's fun to take a trip and enjoy your citizenship before shampoo, hair straighteners, and sculpting clay step in to mess things up.

But I guess that's what makes getting away from it all so great. I mean, just look at babies of the world with their Always-On Bedhead, sometimes for years on end. Folks, are you thinking what I'm thinking? Yes, **we can learn much from the baby**.

Now don't get jaded in your old age. There are some classic moves to pull it off:

- **No-Time Bedhead.** This is where you wake up late in a panic and barely have time to throw on jeans and grab keys before bolting out the door for work. This is accidental bedhead and may result in worried finger combing on the bus or a splash of water from the bathroom sink later on. Still, you got bedhead all day and that's what counts here. 5 points.

- **Lazy Sunday Bedhead.** You wake up at noon, throw on some sweats, have some good friends over, and play video games all day. Or maybe you channel surf with your boyfriend on the futon or watch a golf tournament with Grandpa. Either way, no showering is involved, so the bedhead lives long and lives strong. 10 points.

- **Just-Don't-Care Bedhead.** Top of the charts. This is where your day involves going out and doing things, but you just don't care about your sharp, sideways bedhead. If you can pull off grocery shopping, going to class, or hitting the mall with jagged, bent-up hair, then you win. Note that this is not the same as Fake Bedhead, which involves applying a series of creams and lotions in an attempt to give yourself bedhead-looking hair. No, we're talking about cruising around town with the real thing here, people. 25 points.

Yes, bedhead is a temporary escape from that **Hair Prison** we all live in every day. Freeing your hair is the first step to **freeing your mind** and freeing your life. When you get up and let it go, you sort of let yourself go for a moment too.

Suddenly Juggling Jane relaxes into cool, casual **Leg Stubble 'n' Sweatpants Jane,** who's more fun to cuddle up with under a warm blanket in front of a flickering TV. And Suit 'n' Tie Sam chills into our old pal Couch-Dent Sam, who laughs at all our jokes, does great imitations, and doesn't take anything too seriously.

Bedhead all day long, people.

Because sometimes it's great to ditch the comb and see what happens.

AWESOME!

Successfully moving all your clothes from the washer to the dryer without dropping anything

Whether you're rinsing undies in the basement of a downtown apartment building, permanently pressing at the local Laundromat, or just tumble drying at home, one thing's for certain: **that laundry room floor is filthy.**

Dirt tracks and dust balls coat the cracks and crannies of the joint, so it's always a tense scene when you're moving those **wet, twisted clothes** from the washer to the dryer.

One false move and your dress shirt gets a **cobweb skid mark** up the sleeve. Two false moves and your black socks turn gray and linty. Three false moves and you're throwing everything back in the washer again.

No false moves and you're laughing.

AWESOME!

Backseat car windows that go down all the way

··

When it's a dark, summer night, and you're cruising around town, bass thumping, head bumping, rocking out in the backseat, let me ask you something: What feels nicer than slipping your hand out the window and letting that cool breeze wash right over you?

If you said, **Not much, baby**, then you got it.

Listen up, Auto Industry—to get our summer groove on we need those backseat windows to drop down all the way. None of this halfway, **quarter-way**, all-the-way-but-an-inch business. We won't have it. **We The People** need that nonstop, all-drop window. Door factories and window makers, you heard it here first: Stop stopping, start dropping.

Because there's nothing quite as frustrating as a window that stops short. Have you ever tried to dangle your arm out a stopped-short window? Welcome to a world of cut-off circulation and **cold, blue hands**.

Backseat car windows that go down all the way make life sweeter. They blast us with wind and let us rock out with our elbows out just like the **front seat crew**.

AWESOME!

Getting grass stains

First of all, getting grass stains means that you were running around at high speeds without proper equipment. Maybe you slid last minute to avoid a **frozen tag** or made an awkward somersault dive at a line-drive Wiffle Ball. Either way, the grass stain symbolizes your large devil-may-care investment in having **balls-out fun**, and that's something worth respecting.

See, boring people, like myself, rarely get grass stains running around because we're always doing it in Umbros and shin pads from 7:30 to 8:25 p.m. on Mondays down at the indoor gym.

Now, when you're just running around full throttle in cords and a sweater until you trip on a rock and fall down a hill, my friend, that is something. Walk home with pants full of grass stains, some **spicy kneeburn**, and mud-caked shoes, and you've just had yourself a great day.

AWESOME!

When you know your TV remote so well you don't need to look at the buttons

Ever tried to turn on someone else's TV?

Brother, we both know that's a **tough gig**.

First, there's the **Brand-Name Matchup**. You stare at three identical-looking black remotes on their coffee table and play Sherlock by matching brand names. You eye the Panasonic logo in the corner of the TV and search for the Panasonic remote on the table. Elementary, my dear Watson.

If that doesn't work, you may have to go with **The Walk-Up**. When nothing turns on, you toss the remotes on the couch in a fit of rage and walk up to the front of the TV to search for the Power button. This works until you want to watch a movie and can't find fancier buttons like TV/Video.

Sometimes you get an **Out of Order Lecture**. Your buddy walks in the room and sees you pushing buttons with Spanish subtitles scrolling across the screen. "What did you press first?" he asks, ripping the remotes out of your hand like puppies you happen to be strangling. "You're doing it out of order!" He might even throw in some sarcastic jabs at the end like "How could the TV work without the cable box?"

or "No, no, no, you have to flip the Input switch on the Universal first!"

If you've felt this pain, you know how rewarding it can be when you finally master your TV remote. You don't see yourself changing, but one day you look in the mirror and notice you've become a **Channel Surfing All-Star**.

First you master **the ups and the downs** and then you ace the number pad, even after the **little nipply thing** wears off the **5**. When you get that, there's no stopping you. Mute, sleep, it doesn't matter. You don't need to look and your TV watching efficiency zooms through the roof. Nobody flips channels like you. Nobody cranks the volume when Mom starts vacuuming like you. And nobody pushes **Mute** and answers the phone in one ring like you.

Nobody can touch you, baby.

You made it.

AWESOME!

When you hear someone's smile over the phone

....

Living in a big city can be lonely.

Friends scatter and splatter in all directions and people dear to your heart fling themselves across state lines, **borders**, and deep dark oceans.

And while calling your friends has gotten a lot cheaper, let's be honest: It's still hard to line everything up perfectly for a long phone call. There are time zones, there are answering machines, and there's the general difficulty of jumping into someone's life for an hour when they're in the middle of living it.

Despite these issues, once in a while you land one of those special one- or two-hour phone calls with a close friend far, far away. If you're lucky, after the first **twenty minutes** of what's new at work, with the kids, with the folks, and with people both of us know but one of us knows better, it might fall into that healthy back-and-forth banter where it seems like no time has passed.

That's the best part of the phone call.

Joking like you're back in the dining hall at college before a long Friday night, chatting like you're sharing a bunk bed and whispering on **Christmas Eve**, and laughing like you're still young and still married.

Sometimes if you listen close enough you can hear those smiles shining through the phone like **laser beams**. And they tug on your heart as your brain lapses and enjoys some great times with a loving friend.

AWESOME!

Returning to your warm and comfy bed after getting up to pee in the middle of the night

....

Blind and stumbling, you grunt and scratch your way back to your **wrinkled sheet cave** after an epic journey through the **frozen bathroom wilderness**.

AWESOME!

Moving up a shoe size when you're a kid

....

Some everyday appliances look like they were recovered from a **flying saucer** at the bottom of the ocean.

Complicated bunny-ear wine decorkers, handheld metal grabbers that lift out garden weeds, and of course that **heavy metal device** used to measure your foot at the shoe store.

But I guess there's a reason for it.

If a **handful of rulers** were just lying around, there would be much less suspense when you moved up a shoe size. Mom would grab a ruler, stick it on your foot, and snag you a new pair of loafers. But with the **Foot-Measuring Machine 2000** from outer space **there is drama**. First the gal at the store has to find one under a chair somewhere, then she brings it over and squats in front of you, then she places your heel in it, twiddles some dials up, takes a breath, looks up, and announces your shoe size.

"Seven."

AWESOME!

Perfectly popped microwave popcorn

We've all been there.

Staring nervously into the microglow at the **fat, puffed-up bag** of popcorn calmly spiraling in the center of the dish like no big deal. But it is a big deal, and you know it's a big deal, because despite the puffbag's **straight face**, there's a minute left, the bag looks full, the pops are slowing down, and you don't know when to pull the plug.

It's tense.

Stop too soon and you'll enjoy some well-popped corn but be left with handfuls of greasy, unpopped kernels at the bottom of the bag. Your stomach will rumble and you'll either stay hungry or pop more and overeat.

Stop too late and you'll enjoy some well-popped corn but some kernels will be burnt, the bag will be smoky, and your fire alarm could have a fit. We don't want that either.

Yes, that's why it's so great when your microwave pops popcorn perfectly. Either you grow to trust your dependable **Popcorn Button** or you slowly master the timing yourself.

How good does it feel when you pull out that perfect, steaming bag and pour it in a big bowl as the movie starts?

AWESOME!

That one really good pen that never gets lost

You know the one.

The cap is long gone, **the end is chewed up**, but that trusty ballpoint, she keeps flowing like Niagara Falls.

Loyal, failsafe, and **inky to the bone**, that one really good pen might be stashed on top of the fridge, deep in a dresser drawer, or down at the bottom of the **pencil case**.

But it's stashed, and it's handy, and it does the deed just fine.

Now sure, once in a while you might even think you've lost your trusty old pen. You don't see her for a few weeks, maybe a few months. You figure she accidentally rolled under the stove, mistakenly got garbaged, or worse—was hoodwinked by a callous and immoral **Pen Thief** masquerading as a fiddle-dee-dee, aw-shucks **Pen Borrower**.

There is a **period of grieving**, but one random day you just find her again, sure enough—sleeping soundly in your winter jacket pocket or lounging around carefree in the old Scrabble box. It always seems to happen when you least expect it.

And isn't there just something about that one really good pen that's always kicking around? Yes, in these days of kitchen whiteboards, visual voicemail, and text messages, it's nice having a steady-eddy pen by your side. Because that pen is something real. Something honest.

And something worth loving.

AWESOME!

When you're driving late at night on an empty gas tank and a gas station appears on the horizon

When it's late at night on a lonely road and your fuel gauge starts **flirting with the Big E**, it's gut-check time.

First you enter **Fuel Preservation Mode** and start accelerating really slowly and coasting nonchalantly through stop signs to save your precious remaining fumes. Next maybe you fall into a bit of a **Blame Game**, wondering why you let yourself get to this terrible place and pledging never to do it again. After that it's time for **Survival Mode**, where you make a mental checklist of all the emergency food and supplies you have in the car, imagining yourself building a napkin blanket to keep warm and eating restaurant mints and ketchup packets to survive.

And then finally, when hope is almost lost, with that fuel light burning brightly, **that steering wheel gripped tightly**, and those hands shaking slightly, you drive up another dark, lonely hill and finally notice some blissful heaven-sent gas station lights appearing just over the horizon.

AWESOME!

Remembering what movie that guy is from

Smack dab in the middle of the movie's big scene it always happens.

Everything gets tense for the courtroom finale or **championship football game**, and then all of a sudden the defense attorney or opposing coach turns out to be **that guy from some other movie** and you just can't stop thinking about where he's from.

Wait, was he the prison guard in *Shawshank*? The lawyer from *Miracle on 34th Street*? Or, no, no, no, I got it. He's the knife guy from *Once Upon a Time in Mexico*.

AWESOME!

Using Rock-Paper-Scissors to settle anything

....

While traveling on a road trip across the States a couple years ago, my friends Ty, Chris, and I ended up staying at a hotel that had two beautiful double beds cordoned off in private rooms, and one **thin piece of felt** spread over a hard metal frame in the middle of the common area. Clearly, there were two good places to sleep and one joke of a pull-out bed that came with a free **Day Full of Back Pain** at no extra charge. So we stood in the front hallway and surveyed the situation, bags in hand, stern looks on our faces. We knew decisions needed to be made, and quick. After sleeping in basements and on motel floors for a week, we all finally had a chance of getting a good night's sleep. We had to settle it.

Well, first of all, we gave Chris one of the rooms, since he actually found the place and we were driving his car. It was a gift and Chris took it immediately, without a word, leaving Ty and I to fight over the remaining room. Well, we were through being nice guys. We both wanted that room bad. So we agreed to settle it the only way we knew how—with a **long, drawn-out best-of-seven Rock-Paper-Scissors war**.

Quickly, we took care of logistics. We agreed to shoot on the count of three instead of right after it. Any double clutching would be interpreted as a rock, no questions asked. We ruled out celebrating each win with the ceremonial **action move**, where you snip your scissor-fingers across their palm-paper or smash their scissor-fingers with your rock-fist. No need for any gloating. And lastly, we made doubly sure that it was a best of seven. Nothing more, nothing less, **no extensions**. Whoever got four wins first got the good bed because it was game over.

With that we dropped our bags, steadied our fists in front of us, and sized each other up, cracking our necks and loosening our shoulders for the big game.

And so it began.

I opened with rock, soundly shattering Ty's flimsy scissors. Ty countered with scissors again, falling once more to my sturdy rock. Then Ty switched gears to paper, but I was ready, employing his very own scissors to slice him to bits. Down 3–0 in a flash, Ty called for a quick pause. "I need to think," he said. **And I'll never forget it.** He looked me square in the eye for a moment, squinted a bit, laughed, and then said, "All right, I'm ready." The next three rounds were a nightmarish blur—his paper smothered my rock, his scissors snipped my paper, there were a couple of draws, and then he completed the comeback with a fateful suffocating of my once-sturdy rock with his murderous sheet of **airtight paper**.

He quickly tied it up with that move, and so it all came down to the final toss. Before we threw our fists I peeked behind me at the open bedroom door, the setting sun casting warm shadows across the shiny silk bedspread, a flat-screen TV propped up on the wood dresser, a little loot bag of mini toiletries lying across the fluffy pillows. I looked and I dreamed and I drew . . .

"And a one, two, three!"

Ty took it with a quick slice of the scissors.

I was left holding my open palm in my hands, wondering why I didn't go back to my faithful old rock. I could have **shattered his scissors to smithereens**, and I would have, too. I should have, too. But it never happened.

Ty retreated gleefully to the private bedroom, slamming the door shut hard, sealing my mind-boggling loss with a brain-piercing bang. And so it was. Of course, I couldn't sleep that night. And it wasn't just because of the metal prongs stabbing my kidneys. It was because of the way I went down.

But I can't blame the game. No, Rock-Paper-Scissors was there, settling an undebatable debate. It answered our big question, shutting the lid, closing the door, sealing the deal. **You can't argue with Rock-Paper-Scissors.** When it's over, it's really over. Sure, you can beg for that extension, but the victor never needs to take your bait. They played by the rules and they won.

Rock-Paper-Scissors helps you decide between pepperoni or sausage, the freeway or the back roads, the drive home or the sleep home. It answers the little daily decisions that freeze us up. Who showers first? Who's paying for pizza? Who gets to change baby's nappy?

These are all tough questions. And they are all easily settled with a quick game of Rock-Paper-Scissors. But if you do enter the arena, then take my advice.

Just go for two out of three.

AWESOME!

Pushing those little buttons on the soft drink cup lid

Cola, Diet, RB, or Other.

When we were kids, my sister and I carefully pushed those **little plastic buttons** every time we scored a meal at McDonald's. We pushed Cola if we had cola, RB if we had root beer, and Other if we were sucking back some McDonald's orange drink, which was our usual.

Honestly, we thought there was a big **Garbage Survey** at the end of the day and every customer had to punch their button to send in feedback. We figured some poor sap stuck his arm shoulder-deep in that bag of **lettuce scraps drenched in Big Mac sauce**, hollow ice cream cone bottoms, and greasy french fry containers and pulled out all the cup lids. We imagined he arranged them in **tipsy, drippy piles** and counted how many sold that day, adding the results up on a clipboard and calling them into the head office so they knew how many batches to make for tomorrow.

Kids, huh?

These days every time I enjoy a **fine dine** at a fast food joint, I make sure I still take lots of napkins, swivel in my chair, and press those little buttons on the drink cup lid.

There's just something about the way they give, the way

they turn white, the way they're permanently transformed for all eternity that just makes me itch for it.

It's just compulsive. It's just instinct.

It's just

AWESOME!

Your colon

Have you ever run the last leg of the relay?

If you have then you know it's a stressful experience, because you either **make it or break it**. I mean, you're either ahead and **it's up to you** to hold the lead, or you're behind and **it's up to you** to catch up. Everyone else is done, so they stand behind you relaxing and catching their breath while you give everything you've got to sprint for the finish. And of course, because you're last you're dealing with a sweaty baton, a trampled path, and cold muscles.

It's not easy.

Well, guess who's running the last leg of the relay **in your body**? Guess who's anchoring the team? Guess who's picking up the slack? Guess who's taking the baton for the final leg of the race?

Dude, it's your colon. Or Cole for short.

Now, Cole's a humble guy. I mean, call him colon, call him large intestine, call him big snakey, call him whatever you want. **He doesn't care.** He just shows up to work, all five feet of him, day after day, week after week, year after year. He punches his time clock and starts working in the dark, tight recesses of your abdomen from the day you're born, twisting himself up into all kinds of positions, kicking it into high gear from the get-go.

Now, Cole does a lot of work:

1. **He stores and dumps waste.** This isn't a pleasant job, but someone's got to do it. This man is the garbage man **and** the trash can, think about that. He doesn't get one of the nicer jobs like looking at your food or tasting your food—no, he just stores and dumps it after everybody else has had their way with it. I mean, they've done such a number on it that it's no longer food—it's called chyme, a partially digested semifluid mass that probably smells like what would come out of a dog if you fed it raw pork, chicken curry, and bleach. Thankfully, Cole's a real professional.

2. **He gathers water from the waste.** I know what you're thinking. "Don't my esophagus, stomach, and small intestine already do this?" And actually you're right, that is true. But Cole picks up where they left off. Yes, he smiles backward at the gang, flashes them a big thumbs-up, and then quietly finishes the job when they aren't looking. What a team player.

3. **He absorbs vitamins.** What, you thought he was just a chymebag? Just a water sucker-upper? No man,

he's also rooting around for vitamins too. He's the guy at the dump with an eye on your discarded clothes and furniture, aiming to spot those hidden gems that are useful somewhere else. You know all this talk about reducing, reusing, and recycling? Cole's been doing that for thousands of years. He practically invented it.

Now, Cole the Colon is a huge player in your body, but you'd never know that from talking to him. If you try, he'll ignore you and you'll just hear the deep, quiet sound of chyme processing. And that's sort of the point. He's always there, always grinding, always working the gears, always helping the younger guys along, and most important, always getting the job done. And just try getting him to take a vacation!

So this one's for Cole. Pat yourself on the belly today and thank your colon for being a true servant leader, a humble team player, and a bona fide nice guy.

AWESOME!

The day you first realize you can drive

··

When I was sixteen, the local Driver's Ed course was offered on a muggy, unbearably humid week in the dead of summer. The classroom was on the top floor of an **old downtown building** housing a mixed bag of dentists, lawyers, and travel agencies with faded posters in the windows.

The room had no air conditioning, just windows propped open with rulers, pleading with Ma Nature for some heavenly breeze to keep us awake. We panted and dripped and it reeked like a pack of chalk crumbled like saltines in a big **soup bowl of sweat.**

I don't know about you, but for me Driver's Ed classes were torture. Learning how to drive in a classroom is like learning to ride a bike in a swimming pool. It just makes no sense. Overheads were thrown up on screen, with the instructor drawing triangles to show us our blind spots. We would discuss the **history of seatbelts** and watch gory videos to scare us straight.

It's fair to say most of Driver's Ed class is pretty foggy to me. My notes are long gone and there's no way I could draw you a picture of my blind spot. But there is one thing that I do remember from those classes. One bit of one lecture on one afternoon that stuck in my head. It was when the instructor said that **every driver goes through four steps** on their way to learning how to drive. Rapping his chalk on the blackboard to get our attention, he continued, "It's just a matter of knowing what step you're in."

- **Step 1: You don't know you don't know.** You've never tried to drive a car before so you have no idea you suck at it. All you know is that there are cars everywhere and people driving them. So what's so hard about that?

- **Step 2: You know you don't know.** Surprise! You can't drive. You realize this the first time you make a painfully slow and wide turn into the wrong lane. It hits home when you tire-punch the curb and accidentally run a red light. You can't park, can't parallel park, can't park on a hill, and forget to signal. It's depressing, but at least now you **know** you don't know. You made it to Step 2, whether you wanted to or not.

- **Step 3: You know you know.** After a while it finally comes—the blissful day when you realize for the first time you can drive! Step 3 usually arrives after scaring a few pedestrians, enduring some frustrating coaching sessions with your parents, and listening to lots of "Uh-oh, you're on the road?" jokes. But you finally made it. And now you're higher than a kite, sitting pretty on Cloud Ten. Congratulations!

- **Step 4: You don't know you know.** Eventually it becomes old hat. You're on Step 4 the first time you arrive at work instead of the grocery store on Saturday morning or land in your driveway in a sudden panic because you can't remember the last fifteen minutes of your commute. "How did I get here," you ask yourself, before realizing you must've driven home in a waking dream, signaling subconsciously and turning effortlessly, your brain clicking over to autopilot without letting you know. When this happens, you don't even **know** you know anymore.

But this isn't about Step 4. It's about Step 3. It's about the great joy of realizing you've learned something new, something massively new, and can feel proud that your effort, practice, and determination has finally paid off. That first day you first realize you can drive is a wicked high.

And isn't it a great sense of freedom when the road hockey rinks and street chalkboards of your childhood transform into highways to drive-ins and out-of-town parties? The world seems to suddenly shrink and open up. It's cool thinking how many cities and places connect to the street you live on and all the places you'll eventually go . . .

AWESOME!

Crap job shoes

My shoes go through a very specific Shoe Life Cycle.

1. **Papa's got a brand-new shoe.** Wrapped in tissue paper, wedged in a cardboard box, baby shoes come home from the factory and begin their new life in the closet. Even though you know they're around, you might not be ready to give up your regular pair, so there's a chance they could sit for a bit. That's okay. They're getting used to their new home.

2. **Baby steps.** Eventually they take the first step. It's a bit awkward and they hug your foot a lot differently than your old pair. But they are excited: Shining brightly, glowing whitely, they blind the world with their sparkling laces and reflective sheen.

3. **Adolescence.** Hey, every shoe is going to get a bit curious and test the limits. It's in their nature. These teenage years are when they step in their first puddle, get dripped on by their first ketchup squirt, and go out really late to an outdoor concert in a muddy field. They get a bit messed up, and maybe you worry about them, but they'll be all

right. They had to grow up someday. Some say this is when they first get to know their shoes on a really deep level.

4. **The Workhorse Years.** Now they're number one in your rotation. They're providers of the entire shoe family, putting time on your feet for the pairs of sandals, dress shoes, and gym shoes littering your closet.

5. **Retirement.** Eventually, they hit the golden years. Scuffed beyond repair with broken laces and smooth, worn-down soles, they're put in a home at the back of the closet behind old tennis racquets and a pair of rusty skates. Although they're gone, you and I both know they're always there when you need them most. Mowing a damp lawn, painting a messy bathroom, building a deck in the backyard, they come out and serve as your **crap job shoes**, dedicating the remainder of their long proud lives to service.

Paint splotches, dead leaves, and caked-on mud coat their tired, worn-out bodies at the end of your long life together.

Never ever forget.

AWESOME!

Celebrating your pet's birthday even though they have no idea what's going on

All they know is everybody's snapping photos of them in a party hat and there's a **slice of cake** in the food dish.

AWESOME!

Waking up and realizing it's Saturday

....

CRAP WHAT TIME IS IT I GOTTA GET TO WORK!

Wait a minute.

AWESOME!

High tens

....

High fives are good. High tens are **great**.

Picture it—jaw dropping in slow-motion silence, eye-brows furrowing in mock-angry rage, head slowly wagging side to side, and **both hands** lifting high up top and waiting a brief moment for your friend to answer your call and deliver a booming double palm-on-palm **SMACK**.

Now that's a beautiful picture. That's the happy dial turned to 10. That's a good day giving birth to a great one. That's a photo from Appendix A of **The Study of the Best Things Ever**. Lady, I don't know who you are, where you live, or what you're all about, but I know that you gotta love that beautifully loud high ten and its satisfying twenty-finger crack. It's just explosive.

Like I said, the high five is good too, especially if a baby lays one on you. But really, almost anyone can deliver a high five. It's just one hand! Once you start tenning, the five starts to look wrong, incomplete, and unfinished. It becomes a half, a partial, a sort of. It's like a flop with no flip, yang with no yin, pong with no ping, or a unicycle.

But the high ten! Sugar, let's talk about that high ten. Now **that's** the celebratory hand-on-hand gesture for you and me. See, the high ten takes **guts** for two big reasons:

1. First off, **higher chance of looking stupid**: You throw a high five up there and no one answers it, no problem. You just put your hand nonchalantly back in your pocket, scratch your head, or swipe it through the side of your hair, grease-monkey style. No one notices you covered it up and all is well. But you throw a **high ten** up there and you get left hanging? Well, now you just look foolish—like you're trying to get the wave started at your kid's T-ball game or airing out your pits at the backyard frat party.

2. Also, there's **more coordination required**: Think about it, during a high five all eyes are on that one hand. With four eyes focused on one slap, there's not too much that can go wrong. Yes, there's the awkward pinky-on-pinky slap, but those don't happen too often. Now, the high ten's a different animal. This time each person has to focus on **two slaps**. Time them right. Aim them precisely. Smack them hard. You can't just high ten perfectly the first time. It is very difficult and requires a great deal of training.

However, the good news is that once you work up the nerve to pull off the high ten, it can be a very rewarding slap. So give it a shot. Test it out. See what it's all about. And hey, maybe even try laying a thundering double palm-on-palm **SMACK** on one of your closest friends . . . today! Then maybe go out for beers or something. Wings too, if no one's eaten.

AWESOME!

Seeing somebody laugh in their sleep

It's late, it's dark, it's quiet.

You're tossing and turning, wrapped tightly in a **mummy's tomb** of crumpled sheets, while your bed buddy blissfully slumbers on. Maybe you try lying in absolute perfect silence, flipping the pillow, or taking deep breaths timed to **Subconscious Sam's** snoring beside you.

You might be frustrated, you might be tired, you might be ready to pack it in and scream, but sometimes, once in a while, it's at these perfect moments when the person next to you starts **laughing in their sleep**. And what a bizarre and hilarious sight that is because it's like——**what's so funny?**

I mean, sure, we're used to laughing at things we see in our waking life. Your roommate drops a hammer on her toe, your brother gets squared by a tennis ball, sure. We get those things. But when somebody's laughing in their sleep, it's a different kind of funny because it's **the most inside of inside jokes**. You aren't in on it, and frankly, they aren't either.

So whether it's **the baby in the crib**, your dad in the tent, or your girlfriend wedged beside you on the futon, there's something hilarious when you see them laugh in their sleep and try to imagine what's running through their head.

AWESOME!

. . .

. . .

. . .

Wait, wait, wait, hold on, last question: Do you ever try to **influence their dreams** by whispering little things in their ear and stuff?

Me neither.

AWESOME!

When there's ice cream left at the bottom of the cone

....

My friend Allison was obsessed with The Last Taste.

Sitting on the deck during a cookout, over at a friend's for a potluck, it didn't matter. "No meal should end with anything less than the best taste possible," she'd say, while devouring the **pink and juicy inner cube** of steak she'd saved on the edge of her plate during the entire meal. "It's just not worth the risk."

I admit that at first I found it odd but over time began to admire her strong-willed ability to resist further nibbling. Me, I typically capped off a rich slice of cheesecake with a bite of a cold, tough dinner roll from an hour ago without even thinking about it.

But not Allison.

No, she didn't mask the last bite of a cold cut sub by picking at the stray ribbons of mustard-smeared lettuce lying on the tray. She didn't chase the sticky brownie paste stuck in her molars with a glass of **watery skim milk**. And if we were dining out in style, she wouldn't taste-test a bite of my dinner after she finished her own. "There's no way that could be better than my ravioli was," she'd say, shrugging. "I want to keep tasting ravioli."

So keep tasting ravioli she did. Because that's what Last Tasters **do**, people. They find a taste they like and they stick with it.

Now, we both know Allison isn't the only one. Stop for a second and look at yourself, **just look at yourself**. What are you, lying in bed, sitting on a plane, reading on the beach? And are you nodding along? There are plenty of you even if you don't wear buttons or meet in chat rooms. Basically, if you make sure there's always a perfect crust of toast left for that last smear of egg yolk, **you're one of them**.

But don't worry, because it's a good thing.

See, that kind of **Eat Planning** is something worth respecting and something worth believing in. You come, you chomp, you go home happy, your mouth slowly savoring those final fleeting fumes of deliciosity after the meal is done. Nothing wrong with that.

But sadly, even for those in the biz, it's not all sugar and sunshine out there. No, some foods trip up the best of Last Tasters. Plain nachos at the bottom of cheesy salsa towers, dry crusts at the end of the sandwich, and perhaps most dreaded of all: **the hollow cardboard bite at the bottom of the ice cream cone**.

Oh, I know the ice cream looks innocent at first, and when you start eating everything is smooooooooth sailing. That napkin-clad cone lands in your hand and you give a few light licks, not wanting an **overly aggressive tongue** to topple the tower onto the sidewalk. Then your scoop settles into the cone's lippy grooves and you get a bit more pushy. Broad, sweeping swirls do laps, and sometimes you even punch in with a big bite or a **lip-smearing kiss**. If it's dripping there's no time for small talk because you're spinning the cone like a corncob.

Sitting on a picnic table by the dorms, **watching the sun dip down at the cottage**, camping in the backyard with the grandkids, you lose your sense of time and just keep licking, licking, licking, licking.

Frozen nirvana makes you woozy and lowers your defenses until you're almost done. And that's when it hits you like a hammer: **Brother, you're not going to make it.**

Shocked, you stare down at the cone in your hand and notice it's feeling a bit light. There's more ice cream in there but **not much**, and you have a funny feeling those last few bites of cone are going to be hollow and tasteless if you don't do something about it.

So you weigh your choices:

- **Option 1: The Vacuum.** With time running out, some people cut their losses and form a Perfect O with their mouth and speed-suck the remaining creamy plunder from the cone. This way you end up with a solid 100 percent ice cream finish and ditch the cone in the trash.
- **Option 2: The Pusher.** Here your tongue gets in the game and pushes the ice cream down and down

deeper into the cone. You're not giving up, you're not sacrificing, you're just making sure you end up with a great final taste. The earlier you perform The Pusher, the better for everybody involved.

Now it's a tough choice, but I recommend you go for The Pusher. Don't give up. The benefits are really worth it. I mean, it's a great **last taste** when you're holding that **tiny little goblet** of bubbly, melted ice cream and can toss it back for a tasty cool and creamery finish. Instead of having empty and brittle cardboard fouling up your mouth, you score a soft and sweet sugary delight.

People of the world, let's face it: When you ace this move, you become the true **dairy queen**.

AWESOME!

Sweatpants

Old, faithful sweatpants.

So comfortable yet so risky for wearing out of the house. Seriously, how many of you pull off **The Sweatpant Look** at the movies or grocery store? I bet not too many, despite the fact that sweatpants are **God's Gift to Legs**.

They're just so practical:

- **No need for a belt.** You just toss em on and you're good to go. Just think, if we all switched to sweatpants we'd render the belt obsolete. No more belts! Gone, just like that, forever replaced by a superior technology: the elastic waistband.
- **Easy to turn into shorts.** You roll them up and you're good. That's right: instant shorts. Now that's flexibility. A side benefit is that they don't look terrible, unlike rolled-up dress pants or rolled-up tight white jeans.
- **Stretchiness.** Have you ever heard someone say, "I lost thirty pounds! I had to buy all new clothes!" Me too. And have you ever heard someone say, "There was a sale on Ben & Jerry's last week and

now none of my clothes fit me!" Me neither, but you know that's going on too. The point is that most clothes aren't stretchy, so if the size of you changes, so does the size of your clothes, which generally means going out to buy more. But guess what? You don't need to buy new sweatpants! They're the caring, understanding, stretchy friend in your closet. They'll wrap themselves around you comfortably no matter what size you are. Thanks, sweatpal.

- **Warmth.** Hey, when you're walking around in your beltless shorts, it's easy to overlook one of the key features. That's right, folks, I'm talking about warmth. I mean, there's a reason they're not called shiverpants.

- **Relatively cheap.** What's up with the price of pants? You'd think we were buying limited-edition bald-eagle-head-encrusted-cashmere-infused-Kobe-leather trousers judging by the price of these things. I mean, they're pants! Let's keep them affordable. That's why it's all about sweatpants. A side benefit is that they rarely change color or style, so you can use them for years to come without worry. Remember, when it comes to sweatpants, gray **is** the new gray.

So let's sit back and smile a slow smile, nod a slow nod, and clap a slow clap. Let's raise our drinks, then clink them, then drink them. Yes, let's give cheers to sweatpants. Let's say thank you, sweatpants, for everything you do, on behalf of the world's hot, comfortable legs.

AWESOME!

Multitasking while brushing your teeth

....

Hey, there's a lot to get done around here.

Oh what, you thought those magazines **on top of the toilet** were going to organize themselves? Sure, sure. And I suppose the shower curtain will magically get pulled out and straightened by the same **invisible bathroom butler** too, right?

No, but seriously though: Isn't it all about **maximizing time** while you're scraping away at your pearly yellows? I mean, you master the basic motions after the first few hundred practices, and then it's like hey, hey, couple minutes of free time every night during the big brush. If this sounds like you, then congratulations: You may be a **Toothpaste Stroller**.

Toothpaste Strollers don't worry because they know **their molars aren't going anywhere**, so they check email, set the alarm clock, or put on pajama bottoms while brushing away.

Now, if you're like me, whatever you do while brushing your teeth ends up taking much longer than normal. **But that's part of the fun.** I mean, say you're taking off your socks with one hand while brushing with the other—well, that's like two minutes of awkward hopping and peeling while your brushing loses focus and maybe slips out of your mouth a few times. You end up grabbing the counter before you slip, a **half-peeled sock on your foot** and foamy streaks on your chin, and you just have to laugh.

Because you'll get it eventually.

When you do, you'll be an official member of the **Toothpaste Stroller Society** (TSS). Fellow members, you know what I'm talking about. You know that multitasking while brushing scratches a small part of your brain the right way. Now instead of daydreaming or examining your wrinkles in the mirror, you can feel satisfied that as you spit that bubbly foam puddle into the sink, the dog-eared pile of magazines are just as organized and ready for bed as you are.

AWESOME!

The Parking Lot Pull Through

Backing out of parking spots is no fun.

Turning side to side, checking mirrors, reversing real slowly, you're sizing up how far away your car is from another one. It's an awkward three, four, five-point turn, as you **twist your spine up**, scrape your tires up, dent a fender up, and barely avoid nailing a grocery cart up.

It's a risky, twisty game of **Lot Danger**.

So take no chances and go for that beautiful **Parking Lot Pull Through**, a classic parking move that lets you drive right in and drive right out. The trick to pulling it off is finding a double-empty parking spot, entering it, and then driving up into the second spot.

And it's great because you get two **smirky, satisfied smiles** for the price of one. When you nail that PLPT, you're loving it. When you return to your car and drive out, you're loving it again. For those of you keeping track at home, that's two awesomes for the price of one.

AWESOME!

AWESOME!

Looking at the clock and seeing that it's 12:34

When this happens it's like your day is winking at you. It sort of feels like all the **mysteries of the world** are about to unfold before your eyes as the universe puts up its hand and says "Hey, stop for a second!"

Also applies to 11:11.

AWESOME!

The smell of books

When I was a little kid my mom read to me before bed.

Actually, I suppose read **with** me would be more accurate. See, we had a deal. She read the left page and I struggled to slowly read the right, moving my finger over the words, letting her help me pronounce the big ones.

Over time we worked our way through many old collections from garage sales, bookstores, and libraries near our house. We learned about the lives of Mr. Men, **Curious George**, and The Berenstain Bears.

Sometimes we went to the bookstore on Saturday mornings for a treat.

I always loved walking on those creaky wooden floors, loitering at the big magazine rack, and chatting with the friendly staff covered in glasses, beards, and thick wool sweaters. I would sniff up that heady bookstore air full of **fresh paper**, cardboard boxes, binding glue, and lingering coffee fumes.

The smell of books reminds me of late nights cramming for biology exams between the library stacks at college. It reminds me of lying on my elbows on a **warm beach towel** by the ocean on summer vacation. It reminds me of the heavy set of encyclopedias in my living room when I was a kid, the ones I relied on to write last-minute reports on the praying mantis, Nigeria, or the **1972 Summer Olympics**.

The smell of books reminds me of learning to read and learning to explore the world.

I love walking quietly through bookstores and thinking of how many stories lie hidden in the pages right beside us. Entire lives have been poured into mapping the Earth and conducting experiments, crafting mysteries and teaching languages, showing us how to cook and garden, and sending us on faraway trips to faraway worlds.

The smell of books is the smell of us all coming together to document, entertain, and explain things for ourselves now and forever. It's a big sniff of humanity, a big sniff of wisdom, and a great big sniff of

AWESOME!

Getting in a line before it gets really long

....

Lineups are everywhere.

There are short ones, fast ones, straight ones, and curly ones. Can you stomach the **Top Five Killers**? If not, look away, look away:

5. **Airport security.** Plastic bins, loafers, key chains, and laptops fly in all directions in the maddening chaos of the airport security lineup. Grannies get the beepdown and guards tear through purses looking for Terrorism, while folks jostle about awkwardly, emptying and refilling pockets, a sweaty feet smell hovering over everything.

4. **The bank at lunchtime on Friday.** Even if you only want the machine, chances are good you'll get stuck behind someone making four deposits.

3. **Wherever you get your driver's license renewed.** Throw mugshot photos and a few eye exams in the mix, and that lineup just wraps around and around and around all day.

2. **The bathrooms right after a movie lets out.** How bad is it when the line reaches right up to the inside of

the bathroom door but no farther? Then you're the one opening that door to find a clump of fidgety folks wedged tightly in that **Bathroom Lobby** with their arms crossed and their faces scrunched up. It's a sardine tin of heavy bladders and dark clouds. Not a great scene.

1. **Post-Christmas returns line.** This is the worst of all. Honestly, you may as well keep that ice cream maker and novelty wine bottle opener at this point. Give up, go home, and drown your sorrows in a bottle of shiraz and a bowl of warm, runny orange sherbert.

So yeah, there are some terrible lines out there. Sometimes you beat them, sometimes they beat you, but one thing's for sure: It's great when you enter a classically long and winding line **just before** it gets long and winding.

Yes, when you're first through the **maze of velvet ropes**, when you beat the lunch rush at the sandwich place, when you score the employee who just came off break at the DMV, well—doesn't it feel like **you bucked the system**?

You can hardly believe your luck as you look back at the poor souls waiting. Smiling sadly, you shake your head because you know you'll be there again one day.

But this time you won the game, **you're riding high**, and you're feeling so completely

AWESOME!

Getting into a bed with clean sheets after shaving your legs

....

Stubble-free legs and cool, clean sheets combine to form a silky-smooth ride into **Dreamland**.

Or so I've heard.

AWESOME!

The Gas Arrow

....

Put your hand up if you've ever driven your car up to a gas pump only to notice after you've parked that your gas cap is on the other side.

My brother, if your hand is up right now, you are not alone.

See, some cars I've driven have the ol' gas hole on the starboard side and some on port. Due to my unfortunate affliction with **gasholenorememberititis**, I'm always parking the car the wrong way. Sure, I try desperately to notice the little gas-cap bulge in the side mirror when I pull up, craning my head wildly in both directions, and generally **pretty sure** I caught a quick glimpse of it as I pull in. But then I get out, notice I messed up, pound my fist on the trunk, and pull an awkward seven-point turn before anyone moves in to steal my spot.

It is a terrible thing.

But guess what? High tens around the room because there is hope for **People Like Us**. Shockingly, I have recently discovered **The Gas Arrow**! Yes, believe it, driving fans, because it truly exists. **The Gas Arrow is a tiny little arrow right beside the picture of the gas pump, which tells you which side your car's gas hole is on!** I know, it's crazy. And my guess is that whoever is responsible for marketing really dropped the ball on this one, because nobody I asked (n=3) has even noticed this before!

Yes, just look at that Gas Arrow, head nodding casually to the left or the right, a classy pal trying to tip you off real subtle like. It's a flashlight in a storage closet or a lighthouse on a foggy pier: The great, noble Gas Arrow, telling you which way to park your stupid car.

So thanks for the big helper, Gas Arrow. Until car companies start putting gas holes on both sides or they invent a new wireless gas that lets you fill up through the radio, I think I can speak for all of humanity when I say that we love you and everything you stand for.

AWESOME!

When your friend makes sure you got into the house safe after dropping you off at the end of the night

....

When your friend drops you off after a **lazy, hazy** night it's always nice when they sit with their engine quietly revving till you get in the door. And when you pop it open make sure to wave back so they can **bee-beep** or flash their headlights before quietly drifting away into the dark suburban night.

AWESOME!

Playing with a baby and not having to change its nappy

Save your money.

Babies aren't interested in talking dolls, board games, or baseball. They just want to play Peekaboo, Patty Cake, **Ripping Up Wrapping Paper**, Breaking Your Glasses, or Sticking Their Hands In Stuff.

And playing with babies is great fun.

You don't need to hunt for batteries, **find a set of dice**, or put your shoes on. You just make faces, do baby-talk voices, and fly your hand around like an airplane. They laugh and giggle and suddenly you're a world-class entertainer.

It's great.

Until, of course, it's that time of the afternoon. You know what I'm talking about. Mommy or Daddy pops in, picks up the baby, does the classic **Reverse Angle Diaper Peek** move, and finds a chocolate factory working overtime back there.

When they say, "Looks like somebody needs a changing!" that's your cue to slink off silently to the kitchen. The party's on pause during your daring **Dirty Nappy Dash**, but it's back on ten minutes later when you casually show up and ask, "Hey, can I play with the baby again?"

AWESOME!

Squeezing a little more juice out of dying batteries

It happens when you least expect it.

As you lie on the couch late at night flipping between talk shows and sports highlights, **the volume button** suddenly stops working. So you push it really, really hard until it eventually zaps into gear. But you have to face it: Those remote control batteries are dying. You know it and I know it. And there are only five possible **junk science** moves you've got to squeeze out some more juice.

Here they are in order of complexity:

1. **The wait.** This is what amateurs do. It's called waiting a while and then hitting Volume again a minute later. If this is your only move, then you've got a lot to learn.

2. **Flip-flop till they drop.** This is a simple and extremely ineffective move. Crack open the back of the remote and switch spots between batteries. Give it a shot, but nobody's promising anything.

3. **Ay, there's the rub.** Some people swear that popping the batteries out and rubbing them together charges

them up. "It has to do with ions," my brother-in-law Dee once said with a straight face. Better hope so or you're trying the next move.

4. **Shake it like a Polaroid picture.** My old high school computer teacher taught us that shaking batteries helps move the battery acid around and gets them working again. I didn't say he was a good teacher. You risk looking foolish, so best not to try this at birthday parties or in front of an audience.

5. **The Robin Hood.** Let's say the batteries are dying in your digital camera and your DVD player remote takes the same size. You hardly touch the remote, so they're practically full. Donating them to the digital camera and bringing the camera's barely alive organs back to the remote is like robbing from the rich and giving to the poor. If it works you're laughing.

Hey listen, if you've ever scored big with any of these, then I'm right there with you. Frankly, we all try them because here's the dirty secret about batteries: **No one knows how they work.** Honestly, could you put one together? Do you know what's in there? I've got no clue.

If I had to guess, I'd say battery acid is harvested from the bark of a **rare species** of tree in a tiny distant island country where it's the number one export. Though their struggling economy is barely afloat, wealthy battery acid tycoons sip expensive champagne in living rooms full of remote control cars, **talking dolls**, and cordless radios.

Whatever they are, wherever they come from, when you squeeze a bit more juice from a set of dying batteries, it's like you're suddenly **Dr. Frankenstein**.

"Rise!" you scream at your remote. "Rise, rise, rise!"

Lightning flashes in the windows and **thunder crashes** in the distance as the volume bar appears on screen and slowly starts moving up.

AWESOME!

Falling asleep in the backseat of a car late at night on the drive home

Moonlit skies, **stained plush seats**, and a quietly revving engine combine to form a perfectly cozy late-night bed on the long drive home.

Whether you're a baby in a car seat, a teen getting a lift from the party, or Grandma cabbing home from **Bingo**, there's nothing like drifting into Dreamland in that rusty Volvo on the slow and swervy country back roads.

Yes, those tires rumble over empty lanes as headlights pop over hilltops, **warm your eyelids**, and whoosh past, leaving the entire cab pitch black except for the faint glow of the distant dashboard clock.

And if you're little and you're lucky, you might score **valet service**, which includes wearing pajamas under your winter coat and getting carried up to your bed after you get home. It feels so good you might even pretend to be asleep just to pull it off.

AWESOME!

Ordering off the menu at fast food restaurants

....

Ever had a **Neapolitan shake** from McDonald's?

One where they layer the chocolate, strawberry, and vanilla flavors in the same cup, creating a thick, icy, slow-moving **light-brown-swirls-with-pink-flecks** taste sensation? Yeah, my friend Chad was a regular customer of those. Of course, when he was working at McDonald's, he got sick of the regular menu pretty quickly and started tinkering in the back like a **mad scientist** with his coworkers, developing exotic, unstable, and unpredictable meal creations with the ingredients on hand. There were failed attempts, like the **Chicken McNugget Flurry**, but sometimes they struck gold and created a new off-the-menu line extension.

Now, my world opened up when I first realized with Chad that you could order off the menu at fast food restaurants. Since then I've learned about other secret options around. Like for instance:

- **Wendy's—The Grand Slam.** If the single, double, or triple hamburgers at Wendy's just don't cut it for you, go all out and order the massive four-patty grand slam. Also known as the Classic Quadruple or Meat Cube.

- **Wendy's—The Barnyard.** Are you ready for this? Loaded with a beef patty, spicy chicken breast, bacon strips, and a slice of cheese between each layer, this one's perfect for frat hazings.
- **Starbucks—The Short Cup.** Even though the smallest size on the Starbucks menu is a Tall they do offer a secret Short size behind the counter. Perfect for that between-coffee-breaks coffee.
- **Starbucks—The Red Eye.** A cup of coffee with a shot of espresso dumped in. Now, I'm not a huge coffee drinker, but apparently you can even upgrade this to two shots, which is called a Black Eye. I presume upgrading to three shots is called a Jumpy, Unblinking Eye.
- **Subway—The Quesadilla.** Late at night, the staff might whip one of these up for you if you're lucky. Chicken, cheese, and veggies pancaked between two wraps and popped in the oven.
- **Subway—The Pizza Sub.** Apparently this one's like Sasquatch. There are scattered sightings everywhere and some grainy videos that may have been tampered with. While we're at it, another favorite from Subway is simply **the old cut**, where they dig a trench in your bread instead of just

slicing it, leading to better cold cut and veggie distribution. Also known for causing **The Wing Effect**, where your bologna hangs out the sides of your sandwich for some tasty pre-nibbles.

- **In-N-Out Burger—Animal Style Hamburger.** The well-known "secret menu" at In-N-Out features this heavenly gem—their regular burger patty cooked in mustard, then topped with extra pickles, extra spread, and grilled onions. For bonus points try Animal Style Fries too.

- **Most Fish & Chip places—Batter Bits aka Scraps.** I knew a girl who was all over these. She'd lean over the counter with a guilty whisper and the cashier would nod slowly and hand over a wet, greasy paper bag full of batter drippings that fell in the oil by accident. Yeah, this is the bottom of the barrel of off-the-menu stylings. I didn't say it was pretty out there.

- **McDonald's—The Flavor Saver.** This one isn't that common, but it's where the very nice employee pumps a shot of hot caramel or fudge in the bottom of your ice cream cone. Last Tasters go nuts for this, as you can imagine.

- **McDonald's—Fries with Big Mac Sauce** (pictured). Lots of people put fries right on the burger, which I agree tastes delicious. But this technique allows you to switch things up a bit and put some of your burger's best feature **right on your fries**. Ignore protests from your arteries and ask for a little cup of Mac Sauce on the side for dipping.

- **McDonald's—Big Mac with McChicken or Quarter Pounder patties** (pictured). The bun-heavy Big Mac surgically altered into a meat-heavy Half Pounder or Big McChicken. Now you're much less likely to get that dreaded All-Bun first bite.

Now, I'm sure there are hundreds of other off-the-menu gems that I've never heard of or know about. But that's the beauty! There are all these little surprises just waiting to be discovered. What possible **fast food mouth love** will you discover next?

Ordering off the menu at fast food restaurants is a great deal. Maybe you're a loyal customer looking for that new taste. Maybe you have strict dietary restrictions, so it's either off the menu or no menu at all. Or maybe you're just a grumpy guy who makes personal requests with a **deep scowl and a few thumping cane stomps**.

But whatever the case, whatever your background, whatever your taste, I think we can all agree that it sure is nice getting a little something special for lunch now and then.

AWESOME!

Paying for something with exact change

....

Feel this pain: You're a cashier in a busy store at holiday season.

Now, say you're good at your job and you've been there a while. You've long memorized the produce codes and you bag like a champion. **You're keeping up with the traffic**, whipping customer after customer through the till in no time flat. You're rocking the credit cards, you're rocking the debit cards, and your line is the most sought-after line at the store.

Yes, it seems like nothing can stop you. You are **Cashatron**, a top-secret beta-version prototype of the world's most highly efficient cashier.

And if you've been there before, if you've ever cashed and cashed hard, if you've lived the cash life and have the **varicose veins** to prove it, then you know what I'm talking about. And you also know the one thing that can trip you up. Yes, you know the stick in the bike spokes for a veteran cashier is simply . . .

. . . running out of change.

It happens all of a sudden too. One moment you're whipping through the line, and then suddenly you stare up at a customer and apologize profusely as you awkwardly dump two handfuls of sweaty coins in their hands. You look back at the long line and just hope somebody else **opens up a new lane** while you wait for change to arrive. It's a terrible feeling. And it makes us ol' cashing veterans **shudder** just thinking about it.

And that's why it's so great for cashiers when someone pays with exact change. As an added bonus, customers get to empty their pockets and lighten their loads. Yes, it's a win-win situation.

Plus, there's a **Bonus Round** too! That's when you pay for something with exact change . . . **with every single coin you have in your pocket**. I'm talking about when you have eight coins in your pocket that add up to 74 cents and the bill comes to $5.74. Nope, no breaking a ten for you, because you just won the Bonus Round jackpot.

Paying for something with exact change, folks.

AWESOME!

Absolute perfect silence

AWESOME!

The first shower you take after not showering for a really long time

Sure, the first couple days of not showering have a bit of a **dirty-cool** hippieish roughing-it feel to them. You come into your own, letting the deodorant wash away, your hair get full of **scraggly knots**, and the sweat dry into your clothes. If you're camping, you're at one with nature. If you're at home, you're at one with a lazy weekend. If you're traveling, you're at one with delayed multiple-stopover international flight.

Either way, you're at one in your **dirty Zen moment**. And that's cool.

But whether it's a day, two days, or even a week later, it eventually hits you: **You need a shower, bad.** And you ain't gonna get one till you get home. Suddenly, you don't want to be a hippie no more.

Then you start thinking about it. And you keep thinking about it. You start to notice **dirt stains** building up on your arms and legs. You smell the thin film of leftover bug spray and sunblock on your skin. You comb a **dead earwig** out of your hair while collecting sticks for the campfire. Your scalp gets really, really itchy. And let's be honest: Your **groin region** isn't in the best shape either.

Yeah, that's why the first shower you take after **not showering for a while** feels so good. You can actually feel the dirt washing off you. The white bar of soap turns a bit darker, and you use a week's worth of shampoo to work your hair into a massive **Lather Afro**. The shampoo gets in your ears, but you don't mind. There's sand in there anyway. Your sunburns and scrapes get washed out. Your tightly wrenched neck gets massaged by the warm water. Your nose gets a good blowing. And you wash all the bits of spiderweb, **campfire ash**, and lake algae off your face.

Then you're finally back.

Fresh, sparkly, and squeaky clean, you've completed your soapy metamorphosis back into the old **Clean You** we remember. Yes, your hair is shining, your skin's soft and streak-free, and your scalp is rehydrated and ready to rock. Plus, let's be honest: That groin region is now totally . . .

AWESOME!

The smell of gasoline

Tell me something: Have you ever rolled down your window at a gas station to catch some hot whiffs? While pumping gas, have you ever **spilled a few drops** on your shirt for a little bit of free take-out smell? Baby, I know you're with me. Because you know that the smell of gasoline is one of life's simplest pleasures.

Now, I know a lot of people out there seem to think the smell of gasoline ain't great for your brain. They insist you're **fritzing out all your head circuitry** with these evil airborne hydrocarbons, the equivalent of releasing a sack of rats into a restaurant kitchen or pouring a can of Coke into your laptop air vent. And you know what? **Maybe they're right.** I do fully agree that huffing gas fumes is really bad for you. That's really not debatable. But the regular ol' smell of gasoline just lingering around the fill-up station? I say the jury's still out on that one.

Don't get me wrong: I have no idea why, when my dad pulled our old wood-paneled station wagon up to the Shell pumps, I loved to get out and take a giant sniff of that hot, gassy air. But I know I did. Maybe I felt a bit like a woodsman stepping out of his cabin holding a cup of coffee, a baker pulling a tray of **hot buttery croissants** from the oven, or a wine taster swirling a fat glass of merlot before the big sniff.

Maybe for a kid growing up in the suburbs, the smell of gasoline at the local pumps was the same sort of deal. Just one of those great smells of life. A smell that says something about who you are. Something about where you come from.

Something . . . about what you believe in.

AWESOME!

Your pillow

Back one day on a long road trip, I sat in the driver's seat, Ty sat **shotgun**, and Chris sat in the back. We were trucking down a long stretch of red rocky highway in New Mexico in silence when **out of nowhere** Ty suddenly turned to me and said, "Hey, how long have you had your pillow?"

You kind of roll with the random questions on road trips, because if you don't you'll get mighty sick of **I Spy** and the four mix tapes you brought along pretty quick. So I thought about it for a moment, then said earnestly, "You know, I can't remember ever **not** having my pillow. I think I've had it for like **twenty years** or something. It's completely old, worn-out, flat, and **stained**, but I've had it forever and I can't find another good flat pillow like this, so I'll probably keep it until it disintegrates or until I lose it or something."

I continued to stare straight ahead and fiddle with the radio, but Ty stared back at me **completely horrified**. His jaw dropped, his brain boggled, and he was silent for a minute. "You know," he started eventually, his eyebrows furrowed in real concern and his head bobbing in little nods, as if convincing himself that despite the severity of the news he was about to deliver, it was important to just get it out, "you're not supposed to keep any pillow for longer than a year. It's actually really, really bad for you."

"Whatever," I countered, eventually settling on a radio station, "It's just a pillow."

"Yeah, that's the thing," Ty counter-countered. "It's not **just a pillow** at that point. It's a really dense collection of years of dandruff, dead skin, **dust mites**, and drool. Seriously, it's less 'pillow' and more 'your disgusting head' at that point. It's full of years of bacteria. Bacteria that's had a chance to grow and build cities! I swear, I saw it on the news."

There was a pause, before I eventually dismissed Ty's claim with finality. "Pshhhhhh," I concluded, **putting on my sunglasses** and turning up the volume on the radio.

Defeated, Ty let it go, preferring to let me suffer the **nightmarish consequences** of sleeping on my pillow rather than waste any more effort trying to convince me that I needed an upgrade. So we drove on in silence, watching the world go by on that long stretch of highway.

I let it drift away then, let it disappear, but really—the truth is that I just didn't want to think about it.

No, I didn't want to contemplate the possibility that I might need to replace my pillow. Because there's really nothing like the comfort provided by **your pillow**, is there? I'm talking about the one you sleep on every night. The one that has bent and shaped itself around your head, has been fluffed and squished and packed and flipped. It's **a bit yellow**, there's some hair on it, but it just . . . knows you. It loves you. And it's been loving you eight hours a day since you can remember.

I once heard a stand-up comic describe his pillow as looking like a **bandage from the Civil War**. And mine's probably at that level too. I even think of it as a bandage, cradling and caressing my worn-weary head, providing a gentle escape from reality every night from dusk till dawn.

I mean, that's why I can't get a good night's sleep anywhere unless I take my pillow along. I admit it looks funny walking in the door with a pillow under my arm, but oh well. See, what if I sleep over at your place and you toss me one of those flimsy sack pillows that feel like they're stuffed with fifty ripped-up handfuls of **industrial-grade Styrofoam**? And I'm not taking any chances with the hotel's puffy cloud pillows either, or those wacked-out ergonomic jobs that make your head feel like it's sitting on a **wheelchair ramp**.

No, it's all about your pillow, yours, **your** pillow. I mean, have you ever tried to switch pillows with someone else one night? **It cannot work.**

Your pillow's been there through the highs, the lows, the nightmares, the tears. You've gone through a lot together and you know each other so well. So next time you're planning to crash somewhere? Take your pillow. In exchange for a little less packing space, you'll get a lot more hours of late-night comfort and **moonlit, subconscious bliss**.

And hey, if you don't believe me?

Sleep on it.

AWESOME!

Getting something with actual handwriting on it in the mail

....

Checking the mail can be a bit depressing.

Sometimes there isn't anything in there. **Nope, nothing at all.** Just one big, empty mailbox telling the world that everyone forgot about you today.

Then again, the alternative is typically **a fistful of bills and flyers.** Someone's selling air conditioners, your car payment's due, and the pizza place down the street has a new crust. All nice to know, of course. Just kind of boring, kind of bland, kind of blah.

But that's what makes it so great when **something with actual handwriting on it** turns up in the mailbox. Those little endangered parcels have something very special about them. For instance:

* **Feel that ink.** If you're lucky enough to score a full-on letter, you know how good it feels to hold that pen-scratched masterpiece. Both sides of the paper are carved up and it sort of crisps and crinkles in your hand. That certain texture to it feels very real and honest—like the person who wrote it put a bit of themselves in that envelope and sent

it over. If I were a tree, I like to think I'd be proud if my slaughtered, pulpy remains were used for a letter like that. Seriously, it would bring a tear to my leaf.

- **It smells.** Sure, it may not smell too strong, but the occasional letter has a whiff of hand cream or perfume on it. And really, anything's better than the smell of mass-ironed flyer ink, especially if the ink's real cheap and powdery and flakes off in the paper folds. Then you get it on your pants and under your fingernails, and for what? So Visa could tell you about their new interest rate?

- **The Complete Package.** When you get a handwritten letter in the mail, it has a whole different look and feel to it. It's a complete package. It's a wedding thank-you card in a small red envelope, with a perfectly placed stamp, on translucent tissue paper. Or it's the letter from your kid at camp with the smeared ink and mud stains on it. It's licked shut real tight, there's a spelling mistake in your address, and the letter is folded thick, causing the envelope to puff out at the seams.

- **There's nothing like it.** Because no two handwritten letters are the same. You know whoever wrote it spent a lot more time scrawling it out than you did reading it. And they wrote it just for you, in their personal handwriting, with their pen and paper, and they paid to mail it to you. Lady, I don't care how small or cold your heart might be, you have to admit that's pretty cool.

Of course, the biggest reason why getting something handwritten is fantastic is because it's so darned rare. For most of us, we're more likely to see **Halley's Comet** crash into Bigfoot while he's riding the **Loch Ness Monster** than to actually get a full-blown note from a friend.

So I say treasure those handwritten notes when you get 'em, if you get 'em. And if you don't, there's an easy way to start.

Man, just send a couple.

AWESOME!

Building an amazing couch-cushion fort

....

Building a **family room stronghold** is no joke.

No, it's a kindergarten lesson in teamwork, trust, and the art of war. Follow these six steps to construct your domestic defense:

- **Step 1: Clear and collect.** Get the coffee table, throw rugs, and plastic toys out of the way and begin hunting for materials. Couch cushions are your obvious first targets, but pillows, sheets, and sleeping bags will be needed too. And I don't have to tell you that if your family just got a new fridge delivered, grab that giant cardboard box because your fort just got a den.

- **Step 2: Main construction.** Some people opt for the sleeping bag carpeting technique. Others move directly into building sturdy walls and laying down a roof. Wall possibilities include turning chairs and couches around, tipping coffee tables sideways, or just piling up cushions. As for the roof, carefully toss a few sheets over your castle walls and hold the corners down firmly with Trivial Pursuit boxes, barbells, or an iron.

- **Step 3: Add-ons.** Now it's time to ammo up. Your fort needs windows to spot your enemies, a secret backdoor getaway in case of surprise attacks, and plenty of flashlights to navigate this harsh carpet-burny terrain. Plus, don't forget a TV with Nintendo in the barracks for those long, lonely nights.
- **Step 4: Hiding spaces.** All forts should include several hiding spaces in case of surprise enemy break-ins. Plan a couple behind false wall cushions or underneath a pile of dirty blankets. These also serve as excellent jail cells, where you can trap your victims, give them noogies, and force them to watch you play video games for three hours.
- **Step 5: Rations.** You will need a hidden pile of snacks to get through the day. See if you can make do with a pile of saltines, open cereal boxes, and warm cans of soda. Hey, we're at war here, people.
- **Step 6: Finishing touches.** Finally, it's time to add extra perks like a talking doll doorbell, cardboard periscope, or wide strip of Bubble Wrap under the welcome mat for your Intruder Alert System.

After that, you're pretty much done. Your family room fortress is a tall, plush tower of strength, and you can just crawl in to defend your cozy new confines.

Cushion forts sure do give us a burst of creative energy on rainy days. We get to plan, design, build, and ultimately relax deep in the bowels of our **secret sanctuaries**. After all, it's nearly impossible for kids to get away from it all. Parents watch us in the backyard, take us on family trips, and leave us with the babysitter. Those amazing couch-cushion forts serve as so much more—they're **bat caves**, weekends at the cottage, trips down South, and quiet alone time, all rolled up in a pile of stained cushions, old blankets, and big ideas in the middle of the room.

AWESOME!

Gym pain

....

Believe it, folks: I went to the gym last year. Yes, flabby belly, **spaghetti-thin arms**, bright white sneakers and all.

Though it may surprise you, I am not a walking, talking **hulk of a man**. No, I'm a scrawny knee-pushups kind of guy who spends more time taking sips of water, **talking to the maintenance folks**, and figuring out how the machines work than actually working out. I don't tone my pecs, blast my quads, or crush my delts. If my trip to the gym was a short film it would be called *Stretching in Sweatpants*.

But anyway, my trip to the gym.

It was 8:45 a.m. and I was sipping some water, trying to figure out how the bench press worked, when a steady stream of **spandex-clad seniors** suddenly brisked by me with stern brows and folded towels draped over their shoulders. Honestly, you might have thought there was a sale on oatmeal or a *Wheel of Fortune* marathon about to start at the back of the gym, because these grannies and grampies were on a mission. When I asked a couple maintenance guys what was going on, they told me **Boot Camp** was about to start.

My mind immediately flashed to visions of crawling through muddy trenches in **baggy camo**, swinging over frothy rapids on jungle vines, and standing on the roof of a rusty beat-up car firing a machine gun into the sky with one hand. I can't explain these images, but they compelled me to follow the **Wrinkle March** into the aerobics room.

And I know I don't need to tell you what happened next.

Large, adult-sized Fisher-Price plastic and foam bits were strewn all over the floor, thumping dance music started bumping over the speakers, and a headband-clad Drill Sergeant screamed the sweat out of us. Adrenaline racing, I stepped up, stepped down, and moved barbells all around. I kicked up, swung back, and **prayed softly**. After about fifteen minutes, most of the old folks were barely sweating, while I was keeled over, my mouth sucking back dry, sweaty air, a sharp knifelike pain quietly stabbing my gut. And the whole time **Sergeant Purple Leg Warmers** was barking at me to keep going, don't stop, two more minutes, one more minute, and rotate!

It was intense.

By the end, I was a **Jell-O blob** of hot muscles and shin splints. I felt like I'd fallen down a hundred flights of stairs and landed in a construction site. I was in pain and agony . . . but you know what?

It felt good.

I felt like I made it. I felt like I did something. There was a **tingling buzz of satisfaction** burning in my shredded calves, a lingering ache of pride in the dirt bike tracks riding up my stomach for three days, and a quiet happiness with the gym pain I'd inflicted upon myself.

When you reach up higher than you've reached before, give a little more than you gave before, and dig deep to your core and end up sprained and sore, well, around here we say that's a little something called

AWESOME!

Squeezing through a door as it's shutting without touching it

Tiny squirts of adrenaline pump into your bloodstream when you pull off this classic move.

Yes, suddenly you morph from Guy Walking to the Subway After Work into **Indiana Jones in That Scene Where He Slides Under the Wall at the Last Second**. Your hands stay clean, your strut stays mean, and you zip through that closing door and don't look back, hoping it doesn't nail anybody in the face behind you.

AWESOME!

Snow days

....

Let's break it down a bit. Let's talk about the three main types of snow days:

1. **The Pre-planned Snow Day.** Your town gets hit by an ice storm and four feet of heavy packing snow. It's going to take a couple days to dig out, so somebody makes the call to cancel school in advance. This is definitely a good snow day, but it zaps out all the anticipation. Worst of the three types.

2. **The High-Probability Snow Day.** This is where it's snowing hard and heavy the night before. There are reports of black ice and cars in the ditch. People hunker down by the window with hot cocoa and turn the radio on for weather updates. This is known as a high-probability snow day. You're almost positive it's going to happen, so you go to sleep excited about getting up the next morning. And really, the night before is almost as fun as the snow day itself, because you're already planning the day in your head, putting off your home-

work, and calling your friends. Of course, once in a while the sun is mysteriously shining the next morning and the roads are clear, but this is very rare.

3. **The Surprise Snow Day.** This here's the Mighty King of Snow Days. This is where nobody suspects a thing the night before. Have some dinner, do some homework, brush some teeth, yup—just a typical night around the house. But then suddenly the next morning there's a firm knock on your bedroom door and it's your mom or dad telling you . . . it's a snow day! Now **that's** a body buzz for kids. Homework already out of the way, no risk of missing anything at school, it's time for an all-out lie-back-and-relax chill session with your friends. And the day really can't disappoint because there were no expectations to begin with! You want to sit in the basement and play video games all afternoon? No problem. Build a snowman and shovel the driveways for cash? Sign me up. Construct elaborate forts for a massive neighborhood snowball fight? I'm in. Just be a kid and love it lots.

And so, when it starts to get a bit chilly, let's all cross our fingers and hope for a good snow day season. Let's hope this isn't one of those winters where we put up a **goose egg** on the snow day category. No, I say let's break the record. Let's go for four or five of the suckers. Hey, maybe six even. Let's get **El Niño** in on it. Because ladies and gentlemen, say it with me, if there's one thing we all know, it's that a snow day . . . is a good day.

AWESOME!

The first time you fly alone

Flying can be scary.

First of all, the airport's usually in a distant part of town you don't visit very often. Maybe you snake up a **jammed freeway**, take a special off-ramp, or ride the subway to a nearly off-the-map stop where you exit into a garage full of diesel fumes and shuttle buses.

And when you get to the airport it's not much easier.

Digital boards flash departure times, arrows point in all directions, and winding lines lead to a mishmash of checkout counters. Custom forms need filling, bags need weighing, **passports need checking**, and boarding passes need printing.

Toting your awkward handfuls of documents, papers, and suitcases, you pass bomb-sniffing dogs, security scans, and suitcase inspections. Then there's the **separation anxiety** that comes from watching your luggage disappear on a black rubber belt into a dark tunnel.

It doesn't end there.

Now there are gates to find and fuzzy announcements about delays and cancellations. As you double-check that you have all your forms and you're at the gate for **New York**, not **New Delhi**, you wonder if they called your name, if it's your turn to board, or if there will be enough space for your carry-on luggage when you find your seat.

Flying can be scary.

Now just remember the first time you did it **all by yourself**.

That first time you fly alone is an exhilarating moment. So many things could go wrong, so when you're through with all the documents, **checkpoints**, and security and finally on the plane, you're loving it lots. The flight takes off and the attendant sneaks you an **extra snack** as you tilt your seat back, let your eyelids droop, smile, and flash back at how far you've come . . . at how far you've come . . . you've come . . . you've come . . . you've come . . .

Color-streaked, postcard-faded blurs flash of tricycles giving way to bicycles, of you as a nervous eight-year-old under a big helmet getting **The Pushoff** and wobbling down the sidewalk, your neighborhood opening up into a patchy jungle of parks and sidewalks to be explored. Too big for backyard britches, you teeter down to playgrounds and corner stores far, far away. Licking Popsicles with friends, you find bugs, run up slides, and blow wide open your view of the world.

Flash forward to **the day you first realize you can drive**. After stressful tests and nervous parents, you finally get the keys and explore your town with carefree recklessness. Distant streets and **shopping malls** all connect to the road you're on, and you smile as your hand slips out the window and the summer breeze whips your face. **Burger joints** across town are suddenly close by, and you cruise late at night eating fries with friends as your parents sit nervously in housecoats in front of a flickering TV waiting for you to come home.

The seatbelt sign dings on and you open your eyes.

As you tilt your seat up and glance out the window, just look how far you've come.

Jumbo jets whisk people from Seoul to Sydney to San Francisco as the entire world becomes your oyster. You feel free as you stare out the window and watch your city zoom out to **patchy splotches** of crisscrossed yellows and browns.

The buzzy feeling of pride you get the first time you fly alone is an amazing sensation. It's a sense of growing up, a sense of growing older, and a sense of growing into a confident and capable person in charge of your own life.

AWESOME!

When you spill something on your shirt and it doesn't leave a stain

We've all been there.

Mustard swirls drip from the back of the hot dog, coffee cups splash on the drive to work, and spoonfuls of lumpy ice cream go for a ride.

Yes, we're all familiar with the classic **Day-Long Shirt Stain**, also known as the **International Symbol of Clumsiness**. Whether it's a samosa spill on your sari, a wasabi smear on your kimono, or an olive oil splash on your toga, we all know what that spill means and that spill screams: **You are messy.**

It's sad but it's true, folks. Kiss the job interview goodbye, end the first date early, and skip the toast at your daughter's wedding. It's all over now because you had your chance and you blew your chance. **Guacamole smears** on your tie and **tomato squirts** on your tux just trashed your night and trashed your mood.

Yes, we've all been there. And none of us like stained shirts.

But that's why it's so great when you just barely escape the stain. Yes, these drip-dodging miracles can happen one of three ways:

1. **The Pick-Me-Up.** That lumpy clump of ice cream skids off your stomach straight to the ground, leaving only a couple chocolate chips lying in your belly-button dent. What a save. Just pick the chips up and you're golden.
2. **The Camouflage Mirage.** This is when the juicy beef drippings leaking out of the taco land squarely on a juicy beef-dripping-colored stripe on your clothes. Lucky break because now you can enjoy the day being clumsy in camo.
3. **The Against-All-Odds.** Here's where you have absolutely no right to avoid the stain but do so for mystical reasons that defy all logic. Somebody steals **a perfect nacho** off your plate and carelessly dumps its load on your sleeve, but somehow it just skis off gracefully onto the tablecloth. A full beer gets spilled and drips all over you, but some quick whisking blows it away and . . . no harm done. We can't explain these, but they are true miracles.

A big spill without a big stain means you played with fire and came out cool, hung over the edge but pulled yourself back, and nearly ended it all but instead just ended up being

AWESOME!

Finding the last item of your size at the store

··

It all starts with **The Hunt**.

Mall walking, clothes shopping, you're searching for cute tops or a new pair of jeans. You pop into stores, you do the **Figure-Eight Walk Around**, you pop right out. You pinch fabrics, peek at wash instructions, and hold pants in front of mirrors, bending knees, **biting lips**, and flipping over price tags.

Sure, everything's fine and everything's dandy, until later in the afternoon when you're still empty-handed and your legs start burning, your boyfriend falls asleep on **The Man Couch**, and you get really, really, really, really, really, really **thirsty**.

But you don't stop, **won't stop**, can't stop the walking, just can't stop the shopping. So you keep going, keep plugging, keep trudging along. You keep moving, keep motoring, keep soldiering strong. No, you won't quit, won't split, won't call it a day. You won't run, won't ditch, **till you find something and pay**.

So you keep looking and looking until it finally comes—that moment where you **spot a perfect top** glowing from the other side of the store. You hold your breath, run over to check, and the color looks good, the material looks good, the price looks good, the wash instructions look good, but . . .

Do they have it in your size?

Panic sets in as you begin **frantically flipping** through the hangers. Shoot, XXL, XXL, XXS, XXXL. Suddenly you start thinking you wasted the day. Your calves ache and your stomach rumbles as you ask yourself: Did I survive six hours on a Snickers for nothing?

But then just as the worry is settling in, putting its feet up and getting comfortable, it finally happens.

You find one.

Clouds part, sun shines, bugles blare, and angels sing, as you somehow manage to score the **absolute last item in your size at the store**. Oh, you're buzzing free and your brain flies as you enjoy one of three versions of this classic high:

- **Version 1: Back o' the rack.** Just as you're getting bummed out by all the oddball sizes, you eventually find your perfect shape chilling out in the shadows at the back. Good find!
- **Version 2: Lost in Thread Paradise.** Employees struggle to keep restocking customer throwaways, so sometimes that perfect shirt gets lost in thread paradise. You discover it hanging with the wrong clothes, crunched in a ball in the change room, or lying on the counter behind the cashier. Good find!

- **Version 3: Same solar system, different planet.** This technically isn't the last of your size in the store, but it's still a classic. Here's where you curl up into a ball and start crying big snotty tears on the floor while pounding your fist into the ground until a friendly cashier calls a nearby store and has them hold one for you. Good find!

And now you're laughing.

You grab your bag, stretch your back, and walk the long walk back to the car. Sun setting over the parking lot, you feel energy, excitement, and accomplishment. Now the day feels productive and well spent. You got exercise, **your boyfriend survived**, and you came, you saw, and you conquered.

AWESOME!

When the boss goes
out of town

....

Who's up for a three-hour lunch?

    AWESOME!

Getting out of the car and stretching at the highway rest stop

....

I spy, with my little eye, something that starts with *U*.

If you guessed **Uncomfortably Long Car Trip**, you got it, baby.

Maybe you're in the **Backseat Squeeze** for hours, one leg on each side of the Floor Hump, bladder clenched tightly, holding on for dear life. Maybe you're in a blissful **Game Boy Cocoon,** headphones in your ears, video game in your lap. Or maybe you're driving the boat, steering the ship, mind on the road, navigating steep curves and sharp swerves.

Whatever your situation, it sure feels good when that hot, steaming car rolls to a slow stop off the highway.

That's when you pop open the door and stretch like you've never stretched before. Arms out, arms up, way up to the sky, just popping that back and twisting that neck in all directions while saying **Ohhhhhhh** a lot. Maybe squeeze onto your **tippy-toes** and feel the burn rise up your legs, those cold, clenched muscles getting a **hot slap** wake-up call. Feel your hamstrings stretch long, stretch hard, and cry out with tears of joy as freedom rings again.

Plus you finally get to pee.

AWESOME!

Planning for snoozes

If you're like me, then a war is waged every morning near your alarm clock. It is a never-ending series of epic clashes between **The Awake You** and **The Sleeping You**, with each side sticking to its guns, fighting fiercely in the ultimate battle for the first half hour of your day.

Sometimes it seems like if it were up to our subconscious selves, a lot of us would be lazing around in a world of rumpled sheets and dreams all day. You know how it is—maybe at night you're a level-headed gal with a level-headed plan. "I'll go for a quick jog tomorrow before work," you say to yourself. "Maybe whip up some **oatmeal** afterward." But your groggy, bedheaded self just ruins everything the next day. "Let's keep sleeping," she convincingly suggests when the alarm goes off, hitting the snooze button on your behalf. "See you in nine!"

I don't know about you, but until recently I've been trying to **deceive The Sleeping Me** with the only two weapons I've got: 1) moving the alarm clock to the other side of the room to give my waking self time to get its act together, and 2) setting the time farther and farther ahead to try and trick my sleeping self into thinking it's making me late.

But after years of playing the same game, it eventually happened.

I hit a breaking point.

I just couldn't do it anymore.

So now my new gig is trying to keep everybody happy. That's right: keep snoozing in the picture and **hold down a job at the same time**. Folks, I'm talking about **planning for snoozes**. Adding them to the list. Budgeting them right in there. Finally giving them the credibility they've long aspired to and making them an official **Part of the Day**.

So now I say, if you must get out of bed by 8:00 a.m., that's fine. Just set the alarm for 7:30 a.m. first. Throw your sleeping self a bone and hook it up with three solid snoozes. And you know what, you win too! Those nine extra minutes can feel like hours, complete with vivid dreams and fresh drool on the pillow to show for it. You wake up refreshed, happy, and smiling.

The best part comes later in the day when anybody asks how you slept.

Because you know what to tell them.

AWESOME!

New Socks Day

....

Rip open the plastic wrap, slip off the hairpins, and peel off the sticky tape because it's time for New Socks Day! Let the streamers fly down and the balloons rise up for this magical moment.

Oh, New Socks Day is a terrific **treat for your feet**. We've talked before about how they got it bad. Toe knuckles get stubbed, dry skin gets rubbed, and bunions grow on your baby toe. Squeeze those caked and cracked **pita-bread heels** into tight shoes all day and you'll soon agree: Your feet deserve to be treated like royalty. On New Socks Day, feet aren't forgotten warriors clad in an unprotective armor of dry skin and old socks. No, they're queens cloaked in royal gowns, bathed in soft cotton, and tenderly hugged in factory-fresh fabric.

Also, let's not forget the **Slip 'n' Slide**. New socks grease your feet and let you move with reckless abandon across the hardwood floors of this great land. They let kids dream big dreams of futuristic frictionless worlds.

No New Socks Day chats are complete without discussing that **high-quality toe jam**. What's more satisfying than picking out those furry chunks at the end of the day? When I do the deed, I pretend I'm the world's greatest surgeon, wearing baby blue scrubs, leaning over a sliced-open stomach under bright-white spotlights in the middle of a tense operating room, and then, in a dramatic moment, I just start lifting out bloody pliers again and again, yanking out glass shard after glass shard, as everybody in the viewing gallery jumps to their feet and erupts in cheers.

Could just be me, though.

Hey, now listen: All socks eventually get old.

Tiny holes grow, heels brown and yellow, and elastics fray and rip away. One day you'll hold a warm sock up from the dryer and wonder if your washing machine's busted. That's when you know the dream is over and it's time for you to go shopping.

New Socks Day is the start of that clean dream.

It's the beginning of your new life together.

AWESOME!

Watching your odometer click over a major milestone

When your **bucket of bolts** clicks over a major milestone, you can't help but smile and feel proud.

"We made it, rusty lady," you say out loud, slapping the dash and honking the horn as you sit jammed in the fast food drive-thru. "Happy birthday, you ol' highway roller. Never thought we'd get this far."

And isn't it true: When your car clicks over a **big round number**, it sure is a special day. After all, assuming you cruise an average of fifteen thousand clicks a year, you only achieve this major accomplishment once every five or six calendar turns.

That's reason enough to celebrate.

I'm guessing you probably saw it coming for a while, too. Maybe you were grabbing groceries or dropping the kids off at day care last month when a 99,398 **caught your eye** or a 198,881 made you do a double take. And maybe you made a mental note to get ready. Maybe you wondered where you'd be when the big day came.

Maybe you bought a dress.

If so, I certainly don't blame you, because when your rust-bucket's clicker-counter snaps into new territory, it's like she's

suddenly all growed up. You smile slowly and breathe in fried chicken and gas fumes as your mind rushes back to great times you've shared over the years: the day you first realized you could drive, **locking people out of your car and pretending to drive away**, and hanging your hand out her window on lazy summer afternoons.

Yes, watching your odometer click over a major milestone is a great feeling.

Congratulations on being there for the big day.

AWESOME!

Mastering the art of the all-you-can-eat buffet

....

Munch lunch at a Chinese restaurant, brunch at a **Holiday Inn**, or dinner at a wedding reception, and chances are good you will come face to face with the The All-You-Can-Eat Buffet.

If you're a Buffet Amateur like me, your pupils dilate and your mouth starts watering as soon as you spot the long table full of steam trays and crisscrossed tablecloths. Soon it's game on, and you grab a plate and pile it high with some bread, a few salads, a couple rolled-up salamis, and a bowl of **Wonton soup**. For plate number two, you tackle the main course, scooping up sticky heaps of Kung Pao chicken, soggy French toast, or paper-thin slices of roast beef soaked in dark mushroom gravy. Then you go back for a third plate, this one featuring a tipsy mountain of desserts—maybe some assorted squares, a gummy slice of cheesecake, or **fluorescent pink freezer-burned ice cream** sliding around your plate.

Then as you lie bloated on your chair, your buttons bursting, your eyelids drooping, you face a final decision: **Do you go back for The Fourth Plate?**

The Fourth Plate is always a good idea before you do it and a bad idea afterward. It's the helping after the helping after. It's the **Greatest Hits Plate**, a star-studded collection with the most popular items coming together for the reunion tour, **the last hurrah**, the final dance at the dinner table.

The Fourth Plate is also a famous mark of a **Buffet Amateur**, because it can be the sign of someone who realizes that the second plate was the best and they really just want more of the second plate. For years, I scarfed down The Fourth Plate at the Indian buffet near my college. Buttery, pillowy-soft naans piled high, thick and creamy Butter Chicken, and spicy, simmering lamb in a hearty broth. It was just too much. I caved in every time and walked away with a curry-busting gut and a samosa hangover.

Since then I've been tutored on the art of mastering the all-you-can-eat buffet. Everybody's got their own techniques, but here's what I've learned over the years:

1. **The Walk-Through.** Don't do what I used to do and blindly take a spoonful of everything. No, you've got to do your Walk-Through first. You're a detective popping open steam tray after steam tray, looking for recent fill-ups, traffic around popular items, and sure winners like omelet stations or a guy in a chef's hat slicing big slabs of meat. Now's also time for some Belly Space Analysis, where every item's Tasty Deliciousness is weighed against its Projected Stomach Volume. Bread, soup, and salad rarely pass the Belly Space Analysis test.

Skipping those means you just gained an extra plate and are on your way.

2. **Drink Later.** Sugary drinks fill you up with carbs and cost extra. If you can postpone your Pepsi, you'll save space for the hot goods.

3. **The Sampler.** My dad is famous for the sampler plate. Within minutes of arriving, he'll dot a big white plate with small portions of every entree and proceed to say, "Hmmm," a lot while scooping up tiny forkfuls of each to see what will make the cut. You have to have willpower to pull off The Sampler, but it can be very rewarding. You know you aced it when your next plate is just piles of your two favorites. Good on you.

4. **Staggered Trips.** If you're with friends, don't wait until everybody finishes their first plate before uniformly filing up for a second trip together. No, go separately and act as each other's eyes and ears out there—what's new, what's hot, what's fresh, what's not? Your friends are doing their job when you see them running back to the table to scream, "They just brought out more coconut shrimp!" Also, be sure to designate someone at your table as **The Lookout**. This person should have a clear view of the buffet and raise the alarm whenever they see someone coming from the kitchen with a new steam tray.

5. **Big Plates Always.** Be watchful of the small salad and dessert plates lurking about. Find your secret stash of full-size dinner plates and use them, know them, love them lots. The big plates will let you spread your meal around and avoid piling things high, which generally results in meat gravy getting all over your Caesar salad.

6. **One More Egg Roll.** When the check arrives, take your time. Slow it down and see who still has room. Since you've been so busy scarfing your food and staggering trips, now is the best chance to catch up with your friends. Then after ten or fifteen minutes, someone will likely cave in and say, "Okay, one more egg roll." This is buffet victory.

With these tips plus your personal experiences, you too can master the art of the all-you-can-eat buffet. After that, there's really no stopping you. So eat all you can, my friend.

Eat all you can.

AWESOME!

Finding money in your old coat pocket

My old roommate was sifting through and tossing out some old birthday cards once when a crisply entombed twenty-dollar bill slid out of a faded card from Grandma. Her eyebrows perked up, her mouth formed a perfect O, and she raised her hand up top for a high five, which I promptly delivered.

Finding ten bucks zipped up in last year's ski jacket, lying wet and crumpled in the washing machine, or folded in the pocket of your booze-smelling blazer is such a great high. There may be no such thing as a free lunch, but this sure comes close.

Finding your own money is a lot like **discovering an entirely new currency**, one that cannot be used to pay down debts or obligations, but only has value when purchasing things you probably don't need and wouldn't have bought otherwise, like an old-school beanie cap, novelty ten-pound Toblerone bar, or high-octane gasoline. It is disposable income in the truest sense of the phrase.

For the pessimists out there, you may be saying "Barumph! That money has been all chewed up by time and inflation, slowly losing value and unaccumulating interest while prices ramp right on up, making my life less and less affordable. That found money could have purchased more before I lost it than it can today, so why should I celebrate my own stupidity?"

But Pessy, come on, we're talking about **found money** here—money that hasn't been budgeted for, accounted for, remembered for, promised for, or owed for, anything at all, since you lost it! Surely the few sacrificed cents of interest in the bank are a small price to pay for holding that folded-up bill, right up to the sky in your tightly clenched fist, with no claims to satisfy. Sure, it may smell a bit like mothballs, Tide, or Grandma's skin cream, but that money still works. And it works well.

So let's call found money what it really is then.

AWESOME!

The Laugh Echo

....

While sitting around the lunch table in tenth grade, my friend Mike accidentally squirted himself in the face with a juice box. He thought it was empty and squeezed the daylights out of the thing, causing streams of apple juice to drench him completely. His hair soaked, his eyebrows dripping, his mouth slowly and painfully dropped into a **Perfect O of Shock** while everybody around him rolled with laughter.

For years after that, whenever that crystal-clear image of Mike's sticky, juicy, and surprised face suddenly popped into my head, I burst out laughing. I just couldn't help it. I had a **Laugh Echo**.

Yes, The Laugh Echo is **when you laugh out loud after suddenly remembering something funny that happened a while ago.** It's a random and hilarious event that can occur with family, with friends, or—for bonus points—when you're by yourself in a crowded public place.

Now laughing really is great for us. Yes, it helps protect our heart, lowers our blood sugar after a meal, helps us sleep, juices up our antibodies and blood flow, and gives us mini cardio workouts throughout the day. Honestly, have you ever seen babies just laughing uncontrollably for no reason? They know the score and are probably just remembering something funny that happened in the womb. Folks, you know it and I know it: **We can learn much from the baby.**

So next time you let out a big Laugh Echo in public, just love it lots. Because life's too short, my friends. Let's squeeze in as many laughs as we can get. Then at the end, **when we're old and gray**, when our bones are brittle and our hair is hay, how will it feel when we look each other straight in the eyes and burst out laughing?

I think we both know the answer to that.

AWESOME!

Crying

A study in *Scientific American Mind* magazine said that on average **men cry X times a month and woman cry Y times a month**. Take a guess on the numbers and see how close you are (answers are a-coming).

Now, whether you're above or below average, consider crying a little bit more. When you feel the **hot, salty tears** coming, don't hold back. Let them flood your eyes and pour down your cheeks, because hear me out:

- **Share the tears.** Crying brings us closer together. In these anonymous days of gated communities, big-box stores, and rampant Interneting, sometimes people just need the attention and care of a friend. I mean, when you see your pal crying, what happens? Maybe your eyes well up and you throw them a hug. And maybe that's exactly what they need and why the tears poured out in the first place.
- **Body buzz.** Studies show that emotional crying (versus onion crying or eyelash-in-your-eye crying) actually releases a bunch of wacky hormones that relieve tension by balancing your body's stress

levels. If you've ever said, "I'm okay, I had a good cry," then it could be because crying helps straighten out your chemically crooked self right when you need it most. And let's face it—that's a lot better than holding it in and shorting out your inner gearworks.

- **I'm trying to tell you something.** Babies cry before they talk to let us all know when they're tired, frustrated, scared, in pain, or when they really, really, really want their video back on. The point is that crying is a primal, universal way to communicate and tell us when something's up.

Yes, even though **men cry only once a month** on average and **women let them pour five times or more**, there's room for tears plus, people. So don't hold back because you think it's embarrassing or a sign of weakness, no. When memories of lost loved ones flood back, painful experiences hit you hard, or your heart swells up inside you, I say just let those **big, wet tears** rain down without any guilt or shame.

Because we all need to let go sometimes.

AWESOME!

Driving through your old neighborhood and stopping to see the house you grew up in

··

When my friends Chris, Ty, and I went on our cross-country road trip in the spring of 2007, we managed to stop in the small hardscrabble dirt town of **Paris, Texas**.

In addition to visiting the Kimberly-Clark nappy factory, miniature **Eiffel Tower**, and famous Jesus in Cowboy Boots statue, Ty insisted we drive through his old neighborhood to see his old home.

Pulling down curbless sidestreets on our way out of town, Ty was already in that cloudy nostalgic dream before we even got to the place. "Sure is a lot shadier than I remember it," he commented quietly. **"Trees a lot bigger."**

We pulled up to Ty's old house and his eyes popped as his brain flash-flooded with piles of distant memories rushing back all at once. He got out of the car and started walking around the yard, slowly taking it all in.

Because even though it was just a nailed-together stack of **wood, bricks, and shingles** to us, for Ty it was so much more. And, you know, there is something profound about driving through your old neighborhood and visiting an old home.

Depending on the time and place, you might notice some strange things.

Maybe you wonder if the new family discovered that the side fence door made a perfect backstop for **pitching practice**. Do they know if you hit a chalk square between the outermost boards, the tennis ball almost always bounces back to you?

Maybe you notice somebody trimmed the **old jaggedly sharp evergreen** with the tiny rock-hard berries on it, which was always the best spot for Hide-and-Seek and the perfect burial ground for He-Man action figures when you moved on to **Transformers**. You remember the soft needles jabbing your forearms and dirt sticking to your elbows when you were down there at dusk, and you remember it was worth it.

If you're bold enough to ring the doorbell or take a quick peek in the backyard, you might see a new glass door replacing the **rusty screen one** that always slammed and had that thin sliding metal lock that never lined up properly. Or maybe you notice the same wobbly patio stones that remind you of birthday parties spent eating hot dogs and playing **Frozen Tag** in bare feet on the dandelions and crabgrass. Photos flash and flip through your brain: sun setting over the fence, everyone **licking frosty Popsicles**, mosquitoes coming out and buzzing in your ears.

Oil stains from Dad's truck still dot the driveway and the little handprints you made in the corner of the sidewalk still sit there. And you wonder: Does the dog next door still bark when someone jumps in the pool? Do they still leave the Christmas lights on until late January? Do the kids dunk on the basketball net off the hood of the car?

But whatever you wonder, **whatever you see**, it sure is a sweet head trip driving down those old roads leading to the home you grew up in. You smile and remember summer nights, holidays with your cousins, and couch-cushion forts on Saturday mornings. Maybe you're lucky and your old home is close by or maybe it's torn down or far away, but if you haven't done it in a while and can still pull it off, take that sweet Sunday cruise down **memory lane**.

AWESOME!

The last day of school

My friend Jason had a tradition.

Every year on the last day of school he'd stop on a bridge over the creek on his walk home, pop open his three-hole binders, and dump all his pen-scrawled notes and sticker-covered tests into the bubbling rapids below. Somehow the sight of the papers **soaking up and smearing the ink** before drowning and drifting away gave him the therapeutic closure he needed before summer officially began.

Although not all of us celebrated by polluting local waterways, the last day of school always had so much meaning.

I don't know about you, but our school board didn't spring for air conditioning, figuring we could make it through a few hot weeks before the break. So as the cold winter thawed into muggy summer days, the heat and sweat just **sank and stank**, despite pleading windows propped open with dog-eared textbooks and plastic yellow rulers.

As that last day approached, a certain smell was teased out from all the backpacks, lockers, and gym closets too. It was a musty combination of dodgeball rubber, **cheap floor polish**, acne medication, and locker mold.

But that heat sure brought some excitement with it too.

Calendar days flipped by and teachers taught with a bit

more pep, assignments got a little lighter, and project deadlines came and went. Tank tops came out as flip-flops clip-clopped up and down the hallway, with everybody locking eyes, smiling big smiles, and waiting patiently for that beautiful last day to finally come.

And then one day it did.

And it sure whipped by in a whirlwind.

Maybe your teacher made a batch of **homemade brownies**, and everybody sliced a square out with plastic knives while passing around yearbooks and watching a movie with no educational value whatsoever.

Maybe your school wrote tests and exams earlier, so half the class skipped while the rest played **Battleship**, watched Students vs. Teachers baseball, or just collected their report cards.

Maybe you were graduating and spent the afternoon kicking pebbles in the parking lot and chatting about all the moments you were going to miss as you moved on. There was your first cigarette, getting cut from the basketball team, and the hallway drama of prom season.

Making plans for pool parties, **summer birthdays**, and sleeping in every morning gives you a great rush, and as you walk home with that **pen-scratched yearbook** you squeeze out a small smile and stare way off into the distance of July and August, thinking tall thoughts and dreaming big dreams to fill those beautifully wide open spaces.

AWESOME!

When you're right near the end of the book

You've been through so much together.

It seems like ages ago when you first cracked her open, flipped past the small print **mumbo jumbo**, and read that first sentence. Maybe you knew you'd like it or maybe you judged that first page harshly, playing hard to get, eyeing the others on the shelf, seeing if this puppy was really worth your time.

But then you got sucked in.

Characters grew and a few chapters ended with cliff-hangers that kept you up much too late. You laughed as you flipped and flipped on a long flight, your eyes welled at the cottage, and you cozied up through big scenes under an **old blanket** on the front porch.

When you're **right near the end of the book**, you feel the anticipation pulsing. As you sit still in **absolute perfect silence**, it's amazing how your mind is racing, your heart is pumping, and your ears tune out the world around you. Maybe you put the book down to go to the bathroom or grab a glass of water, trying to guess the ending just before you read it: Will she find her mother, will he admit how he feels, will Gryffindor win the House Cup?

Maybe you savor those last few pages, maybe you race right through them, or maybe anticipation gets the best of you and you flip right to the end. Either way, pretty soon you're closing that book with a **satisfying shut** and adding it to the freshly read pile on your shelf.

Finishing a book makes you feel good.

You're almost there.

AWESOME!

Smiling and thinking of good friends who are gone

I met Chris Kim in September 2005 in Boston.

A tiny Korean guy with thin eyes hidden behind thick glasses under a **well-worn and faded ball cap**, he looked kind of mousy under awkwardly baggy clothes and behind a soft voice. And even though neither of us drank much, **we met at a bar**—me speed-sucking a gin and tonic through a needle-thin straw, him warming a well-nursed beer and occasionally taking **baby sips**.

When he mentioned he was from Boston, I asked about the **Red Sox** and he played along well enough. "Big win last night," he offered cautiously. "Maybe still have a chance at the playoffs?" Of course, that launched me on a rant about the bullpen and whether **Curt Schilling** had enough steam for another big run. He nodded on, listening intently, asking genuine and serious questions, and letting our friendship take root over sports, of all things. Of course, he never watched the stuff, but was nice enough to let me talk mind-lessly about it all night.

Full of wry smiles, awkward pauses, and **mock-serious faces**, Chris was a complex, fascinating, creative person who grew into a remarkably close friend during the two years we went to school together. He got excited about little things, like **caramelizing onions** perfectly for an hour on low heat, getting randomly selected to fill out a survey of his radio habits, or learning a new keyboard shortcut in **Microsoft Excel**.

But it wasn't the **bar scene** that helped our friendship bloom. It was the **car scene**.

Yeah, when I showed up to class on our first winter morning, **shivering to the bone** in a flimsy nylon coat, my hair wet, my face dripping, Chris asked where I lived and if I needed a ride the next day. As I was at that moment toweling my face off with a fistful of **balled-up Kleenex**, I took him up on it right away. (Lucky for me Chris had signed up to be a senior student in an undergrad residence way off campus, spending his free time for two years **chaperoning social events**, holding heads above toilets, and editing two or three resumes a night at a steady clip.)

Anyway, he began picking me up every morning for the next two years, probably at least a **couple hundred rides**, never once accepting money for gas because, as he said, "I'm going that way anyway." When other students heard about my taxi service, they got in on it too. It started with a "Hey Chris, if there's a blizzard tomorrow, can I catch a lift?" and turned into Chris emailing three or four of us each night, giving us the **Bus Schedule**, as he called it, timed precisely to the minute for the next morning. And so it went—us piling into his car after he'd spent the first few minutes warming it up for us, tightly blanketed in fat mittens and his trademark **big blue hat**.

Last year I nervously started up the website that inspired this book, tentatively dipping my toe into cyberspace where anyone could see. Chris of course adopted his Mexican half-brother pseudonym **San Carlos** and peppered the site with comments of support from the get-go. On **Popping Bubble Wrap** he wrote, "I learned on the news that Bubble Wrap is a fantastic insulator because of the trapped air, so if you're cold DO NOT POP IT but wrap yourself in it." On **Paying for something with exact change** he wrote, "I save all my pennies in my car. And then, the next time I do McDonald's drive-thru, I fling all the pennies into the server's face . . . No actually, I put the pennies into the Ronald McDonald's House box underneath the window." On **Playing with a baby and not having to change its nappy** he wrote, "I don't mind changing my nephews' nappies. It only got weird when they began to talk. Awkward!"

I loved his sense of humor and his way about himself. I loved how he laughed, frequently, at little things and got so excited about tiny details most people overlooked. Chris and I spoke three or four times a week after we graduated, in **ten or fifteen minute** snippets usually, but sometimes for an hour or two. He'd tell me about the sourdough bread he was baking that day, the elaborate meal he had planned for friends coming for dinner, or the *New York Times* article he thought I should check out. I would ask him for ideas for awesome things—he had plenty—and occasionally go on long rants about sports.

Chris died suddenly last year. He was thirty-two.

No amount of the usual closing rhyming couplets or **fist-to-the-sky proclamations** are going to bring him back. But I know he's in a peaceful place and would want us all to just be happy, keep plugging, and enjoy our lives as fully as we can. So thank you, Chris. You'll always inspire me.

And you'll always be so incredibly awesome.

Remembering how lucky we are to be here right now

Over dinner one night my dad started telling me about his first day in Canada.

It was 1968 and he was twenty-three, arriving on a plane with **eight dollars** in his pocket to start a new life by himself in a country he had never visited.

"A community group had a welcome dinner for new immigrants," he started excitedly. "And they had a big table of food!"

I was unimpressed.

"A table of food," I agreed flatly while staring straight ahead and flipping past baseball highlights on TV.

"A table of food," he continued. "Basically, Neil, all the presentation of the picnic food on the table, I didn't recognize. There were two or three kinds of salad. Potato salad, **macaroni salad**, maybe coleslaw. Probably four different kinds of sandwiches, ham sandwich, turkey sandwich, chicken sandwich, roast beef sandwich. Then there were the main courses they called it, you know, tuna casserole? Then the dessert was pies. Which I never seen pies before."

I put down the remote and glanced at him cockeyed. Behind the thick, boxy glasses, I could see his eyes darting wildly.

"How did you know what everything was?"

"My brother was there, so I will ask him and he told me whatever it is. The trays of cold cuts was different, instead of regular chicken they have sliced them, sometimes they have them rolled with the toothpick in them. I had never seen cold cuts before, I seen chicken in chicken form but not rolled up. Same for cheese . . . some were in slices, some of them in squares."

"What did you eat?" I asked.

"I ate everything, that's the only way to get to know! I can't believe how many different things you can get here!"

My dad would take me to the grocery store and marvel at the signs beside every fruit. He was fascinated that pineapples came from Costa Rica and kiwis were shipped from New Zealand. Sometimes he came home and opened an atlas to find out where the countries were. "Somebody brought dates from Morocco and dropped them five minutes from home."

He'd just smile and shake his head.

But if I really stop to think about it, a lot had to happen before we could be here right now. A lot had to happen before we could buy bananas from Ecuador and eat turkey cold cuts, before we could flip through books about warm underwear and cool pillows, before we learned to read anything at all, before we grew tall, before we could talk, before we could walk, before we were even born . . .

So let's stop for a second and pull back. Let's pull way, way, way, way back.

Okay.

You used to be a sperm.

Now don't get self-conscious. We all used to be sperm. Check out the period at the end of this sentence. That tiny little dot is around 600 microns wide. When you were a sperm, you were about 40 microns wide. And you were so cute back then too, with your **little tail** wagging all over the place and your love of swimming. Boy, could you swim. In fact, if you hadn't outswum your siblings, you might be a slightly different version of yourself right now. Maybe you'd have a higher-pitched laugh, **hairier arms**, or stand two inches shorter.

You had a great life as a sperm but always felt incomplete. The truth is you weren't whole until you met an egg. And then you two began a nine-month project to make a cool new version of you. It took a while but you grew arms and legs and eyeballs and lungs. You grew nerves and nails and eardrums and tongues.

For a sperm to meet an egg it means your mom met your dad. But it's not just them. Think about how many people had to meet, fall in love, and make love for you to be here. Here's the answer: A lot. Like **a lot** a lot.

Before they had you, none of your ancestors drowned in a pond, got strangled by a python, or skied into a tree. None of your ancestors choked on a peach pit, was trampled by buffalo, or got their tie stuck in an assembly line.

None of your ancestors was a virgin.

You are the most **modern, brightest spark** of years and years and years of survivors who all had to meet each other in order to eventually make you.

Your nineteenth-century Grandma met your nineteenth-century Grandpa down at the candle-making shoppe. She liked his **muttonchops** and he thought she looked cute churning butter.

Your Middle Ages Grandpa met your Middle Ages Grandma while they both poured hot oil from the castle turrets on **pillaging Vikings**. She liked his grunts and he thought the flowers in her hair made her heaving bosoms jump out.

Your Ice Age Grandpa crossing the Bering Bridge in a woolly mammoth fur met your Ice Age Grandma dragging a club in the opposite direction. He liked her **saber-toothed necklace** and she dug his unibrow.

Your ancient rainforest Grandpa was picking berries naked in the bush while your ancient rainforest Grandma was spearing dodos for dinner. She liked his **jungle funk** and he liked her cave drawings. If it wasn't for the picnic they had afterward, maybe you wouldn't be here.

You're pretty lucky all those people met, fell in love, made love, had babies, and raised them into other people who did it all over again. This happened over and over and over again for you to be here. Look around the plane, coffee shop, or park right now. Look at your husband snoring in bed, your girlfriend watching TV, or your sister playing in the back-yard. **You are surrounded by lucky people.** They are all the result of long lines of survivors.

So you're a survivor too. You're the latest and greatest. You're the top of the line. You're the very best nature has to offer.

But a lot had to happen before all your strong, fiery ancestors met each other and fell in love over and over again for hundreds of thousands of years . . .

So let's stop for a second and pull back again. Let's pull way, way, way, way back.

Okay.

Let's go on a field trip. Put your shoes on because we're heading outside.

Take a bowling ball and drop it on the edge of your drive-way. That's our Sun. Yeah, the ball is only eight inches across and the actual sun is **eight hundred thousand miles** across, but that's our scale for this little brain wave. Okay, now walk down your street ten big paces and drop a grain of salt on your neighbor's lawn. **That's Mercury.** Take nine more paces down the street and drop a peppercorn for Venus. And then take another seven paces, so you're now **two or three houses** down the block, and toss down another peppercorn.

You got it.

That peppercorn is Earth.

Here we are, basking in the blazing sun, twenty-six big steps away from the bowling ball. Our giant planet is just a tiny speck in the **middle of nowhere**, but here's the crazy part: It gets a whole lot bigger.

If you keep walking, Mars is only a couple more houses away, but Jupiter ends up **ninety-five big paces** down the street, out of the neighborhood, and halfway to the corner store. By now a dog is probably slobbering in the bowling ball finger holes and kids are flying by you on their bikes, slurping **drippy Popsicles** and wondering what's up with this nut tossing crumbs on the sidewalk, acting out some demented suburban version of Hansel and Gretel.

If you want to finish up our solar system, you're going to have to start taking two- and three-hundred paces for the remaining planets, eventually dropping a grain of salt for Pluto **half a mile** away from the bowling ball. You can't see the bowling ball with binoculars and it's getting cold out for your long walk home.

But here's the crazier part: That's just **our** solar system. That's just **our** bunch of rocks flying around **our** big bright bowling ball star.

Turns out our big bright star and all its salt grains and peppercorns are racing around a cosmic racetrack with **two hundred billion** other big bright bowling ball stars. You'd have to cover the entire Earth with bowling balls **eight thousand times** to represent the number of stars in our racetrack. Did we mention this racetrack has a name? Yup, it's called the Milky Way galaxy, presumably because the scientists who first noticed it were all eating delicious Milky Way candy bars late that Friday night down at the telescopes.

So basically our bowling ball, salt, and peppercorns are flying in the fast lane around a ridiculously giant racetrack galaxy called the Milky Way with billions and billions of other bowling balls, salt grains, and peppercorns.

But are you ready for the craziest part: **That's just our galaxy.** Guess how many giant racetrack galaxies are in all of outer space? Oh, not many. Just **more than we can possibly count.** Honestly, nobody knows how many galaxies are out there in the big blackness. All we know is that every few years somebody stares out a little farther and finds millions more of them just shining way out in the void. We don't know how deep it goes because our rocket ships don't blast off that far and our thickest, fattest telescopes can't see that far.

Now, all this space talk might make us feel small and insignificant, but here's the thing, here's the big thing, here's the biggest thing of all: **Of the millions of places we've ever seen, it appears as though Earth is the only place that can support life.** The only place! Oh sure, there could be other life-giving planets we haven't seen yet, but the point is that Earth could easily have been a clump of sulfur gas, be lying in darkness forever, or have winters that dip a couple hundred degrees and last twenty years like Uranus.

On this planet Earth, the only one in the giant dark blackness where anything can live, we ended up being **humans**.

Congratulations, us!

We are the **only** species on the **only** life-giving rock capable of love and magic, architecture and agriculture, jewelry and democracy, airplanes and highway lanes. We're the only ones with interior design and horoscope signs, fashion magazines and house party scenes, horror flicks with monsters, guitar jams at concerts. We got books, buffets, and radio waves, wedding brides and roller coaster rides, clean sheets and good movie seats, bakery air and rain hair, Bubble Wrap and illegal naps.

We got all that. But people, listen up.

We only get a hundred years to enjoy it.

I'm sorry but it's true.

Every single person you know will be dead in a hundred years—the foreman at your plant, the cashiers at your grocery store, every teacher you've ever had, anyone you've ever woken up beside, all the kids on your street, every baby you've ever held, every bride who's walked down the aisle, every **telemarketer** who's called you at dinner, every politician in every country, every actor in every movie, everyone who's cut you off on the highway, everyone in the room you're sitting in right now, everyone you love, and you.

Life is so great that we only get a tiny moment to enjoy everything we see. And that moment is right now. And that moment is counting down. And that moment is always, always fleeting.

You will never be as young as you are **right now**.

So whether you're enjoying your first toothpicked turkey

cold cuts and marveling at apples from South Africa, dreaming of strange and distant relatives from thousands of years ago, or staring into the blackness of **deep, deep space**, just remember how lucky we all are to be here right now.

If you feel that sense of wonder and beauty in all the tiny joys in life, then you're part of an international band of old souls and optimists, smiling on sidewalks, dancing at weddings, and flipping to the other side of the pillow. Let's all high five and keep thinking wild thoughts, **dreaming big dreams**, and laughing loud laughs.

Thank you so much for reading this book.

And thank you for being

AWESOME!

ACKNOWLEDGMENTS

And away we go!

To the Sun, thanks for giving us heat, life, and pretty sunsets.

To my old campus newspaper *Golden Words*, thanks for being a source of good times for four years at college. Shout-outs to Jay Pinkerton and Mike Jones for their guidance and ideas.

To the *New York Times*, thanks for blowing my mind every Sunday. I just can't get enough.

To Sam Javanrouh, thank you for taking photos for this book. The way you see the world is stunningly beautiful. To fellow bloggers Frank Warren of PostSecret, Jen Yates of Cake Wrecks, Christian Lander of Stuff White People Like, Ben Huh of FAIL Blog, Gala Darling of galadarling.com, David Cain of Raptitude, and Adam Fuhrer of PICDIT, thanks for showing me the virtual ropes.

To Mu, Andy, and everyone at Digg, thanks for introducing me to your wild world. Thanks to Drew Curtis at Fark for believing in old, dangerous playground equipment.

Thanks to many great teachers I've had over the years, especially Mr. Olson, Mr. Mac, Mr. Howes, Ms. Eales, Ajay Agrawal, Mike Wheeler, Frances Frei, and André Perold. Special thanks to Ms. Dorsman for pushing me out of my shell in third grade.

To Canada and the United States, thanks for letting me live in you. I'm lucky to have enjoyed so many years with great people in both countries. Sure, y'all keep fine-tuning these ships, but so much of what you got going on is clicking jussssssst fine.

To all of Section A, especially Brian, Rob, Erik, and Ryan, thank you for the support. To my oldest friends, Scott, Mike, Rye, Chad, and H, thanks for supporting me since I forced you to buy newspapers back in grade school, robbing you of many delicious Hot Lips and Swedish Berries. Special thanks to Chad for his beautiful off-the-menu brain.

To jdurley, Mike Dover, and Freddo, thank you for being a tremendous source of bright lightbulb ideas and great comments. Freddo, special thanks for your rock-solid advice and friendship through everything.

To everyone who has ever read, blogged, commented, emailed, MyFaced, Tweetered, or Spacebooked any part of 1000 Awesome Things around the electronical intertubes, thank you sincerely for your support.

To WordPress, thank you so much for hosting my site from Day 1. You give people all over the world a voice.

Thanks to many close friends who have supported me, especially Dee, Ryan, Gill, Drew, Joey, Alec, Danielle, Roz, Shiv, Arlene, Baxter, Dave, Angela, Bob, Jim, Andrew, Ryan, Kevin, and Agostino.

To Ivan, Matthew, Halli, Amanda, Beth, and everyone at AEB/Putnam and Penguin Publishing, thank you for believing in this from the beginning. It's been an absolute pleasure working with you.

To my editor, Amy Einhorn, you are a million percent amazing. I'm lucky to know you and even luckier to work with you. You're something very, very special, Amy.

To everybody at William Morris Endeavor, especially Cathryn Summerhayes, Tracy Fisher, Raffaella DeAngelis, Michelle Feehan, Laura Bonner, Lauren Heller Whitney, Janelle Milanes, and the one and only superwoman, Erin Malone, thank you for changing my life. I am more grateful than you can know.

To Louis Sachar, thanks for writing *Sideways Stories from Wayside School* and getting a kid excited about writing.

To folded, scrunched-up jackets, thanks for propping up my head when I take illegal naps all over the place.

To Guy Ottewell, thank you for permission to use your Thousand-Yard Model with the bowling ball and peppercorns. For those who like Guy's science experiments, check out http://www.universalworkshop.com.

To Conan O'Brien, Craig Ferguson, David Sedaris, Jerry Seinfeld, Oprah and Ellen, I admire your genius and passion.

To the Webby Awards, thank you sincerely for the recognition. I'm massively flattered and appreciative.

To Jim Davis, Bill Watterson, and Gary Larson, thanks for giving a nerdy kid with a bad haircut laughs before school.

Thank you to Reenah and Dina Kim for your support during this process. And to Chris, rest in peace my friend. We'll all see you soon.

To anyone adding positive energy to the world, whether you're helping folks in trouble, teaching kids to love life, or making strangers laugh, I admire you tremendously.

Thank you, Mom, Dad, and Nina. You gave me everything I've got and this is for you.

Finally, thank you to you. Thank you for reading this sentence. And this one. And this one. Thank you for this great trip together. Please feel free to send me your awesome anytime at 1000awesomethings@gmail.com or PO Box 361, Station B, Toronto, ON M5T 2W2.

Take care, everybody.

ABOUT THE AUTHOR

Neil Pasricha works an office job in the suburbs, eats frozen burritos for dinner, and needs to go to the gym more. He's just a regular guy who loves the smell of gasoline, sleeping on the cool side of the pillow, and peeling an orange in one shot. Visit his website at: www.1000awesomethings.com